MORE SALT
IN MY KITCHEN

MORE SALT
IN MY KITCHEN

JEANETTE LOCKERBIE

MOODY PRESS

CHICAGO

© 1980 by
THE MOODY BIBLE INSTITUTE
OF CHICAGO

Library of Congress Cataloging in Publication Data

Lockerbie, Jeanette W.
  More salt in my kitchen.

  1. Women—Prayer-books and devotions—English.
I. Title.
BV4844.L62   242'.643   80-12357
ISBN 0-8024-5668-5

Fourth Printing, 1982

Printed in the United States of America

For the faithful readers of
SALT IN MY KITCHEN,
*whose gracious and helpful comments
encouraged me to write*
MORE SALT

WISDOM THEN, WISDOM NOW

BIBLE READING: Proverbs 1:1-7

The class on nutrition was in progress when Sandra raised the question, "But didn't you give us just the opposite information last week? I'm afraid I'm confused."

Haven't we all felt like that at times? We've just become used to a new product, or a new approach or procedure, when along comes an expert telling us we need to change whatever we're doing or buying.

It's hard to know what *is* right with all the voices bombarding us. And some authorities have changed their own minds. Dr. Benjamin Spock, for example, admits that his earlier counsel to parents should be scrapped in favor of his newer theories.

Likewise, if we listen to certain people we will be told that the Bible is outdated, that it's old-fashioned to believe God's Word in the way our parents and grandparents did.

Are we to believe, then, that God is learning new things He didn't know before today's world? Is the Almighty just catching up with us in our expanding knowledge?

The Bible *lives and abides* forever (present tense), Peter tells us (1 Peter 1:23). We will never be disillusioned by learning that after living by God's Word, we find it to be outdated, not effective to meet our needs today.

True, we are learning new things—some good, some not so good. It's said that the majority of scientists who ever lived are alive and functioning today. One "wonder invention" is quickly superseded by a new one, as modern knowledge increases.

There's nothing wrong with learning new things. In fact we will never grow mentally, emotionally, or spiritually, if

7

we keep a closed mind toward everything new. The problem arises when we do not question whether the new is better than the old. Nor should we discard our values in the interest of something new. We are told to "prove all things; hold fast that which is good" (1 Thessalonians 5:21). Nowhere is that more true than in spiritual things. God's wisdom, like His Word, is unchanging. It was wisdom when it was given; it is the same wisdom now.

TODAY'S THOUGHT: God's wisdom is not, like today's knowledge, doubling every ten years.

PERFECTIONISM—GOOD OR BAD?

BIBLE READING: Philippians 1:1-6

Sue and Miriam, neighbors, were discussing something they had read on perfectionism.

"Maybe I'll have to change my mind," Sue admitted, "for I've always thought that perfectionism was a good thing to strive for. But now—"

"That piece made me think, too," said Miriam, shaking her head.

Like those women, I had to change my mind on that subject. I can recall when I would have felt highly complimented if anyone had called me a perfectionist. But I've learned since then something of what the trait can do both to the perfectionist and those around her.

The woman who prides herself on being a perfectionist is usually a driven person. She works early and late, yet can rarely enjoy the good inner feeling of having done something well. Always, in her mind, she should have done "better." Unhappily, she tends to find fault with everyone else's achievements, having set for them the same impossible standards she has for herself. All too often that results in her having few friends, for continual criticism is hard on friendship. Another disastrous result is that her witness as a Christian is far from attractive to her unsaved friends and neighbors. They don't wish to be like her, and may attribute her fault finding to what she believes as a professed Christian.

How can we overcome the drive for perfectionism? We don't want to recommend a "don't care" attitude. As God's people, we should have no less than the pursuit of excellence

9

as our goal. But there is sometimes a fine line between that pursuit and negative perfectionism.

Paul offers a solution that provides balance, in Philippians 3:12-14: "Not as though I had already attained, either were already perfect . . . I press toward the mark." The apostle was aware that although we are "created in Christ Jesus unto good works," we are nevertheless imperfect people living in an imperfect world. Only Jesus our Lord ever walked perfectly before God.

There is a beautiful thought being expressed in one of today's gospel songs: "He looked beyond my faults and saw my need." God will enable us—*if we want to* and if we ask Him—to overlook the faults of others. He will help us even to tolerate our own weaknesses rather than being driven by "should's."

We can rest our expectations on Psalm 138:8, "The Lord will perfect that which concerneth me."

TODAY'S THOUGHT: How much better to be imperfect and loving, than to be "perfect" and cold.

WHAT DOES NICE MEAN?

BIBLE READING: Matthew 7:7-12

My granddaughter was in third grade when she wrote me something of her fears about her teacher for the coming school year. "She's new in our school so none of my older friends have had her," Ellyn explained, "and I don't know if she is nice or not."

I found myself wondering what "nice" means to a little school girl. Obviously it was a very real factor in her expectation of her own well-being in the classroom. But what images did "nice" evoke in her mind?

A few days later I had the opportunity to explore that with a child the same age as my Ellyn. We were talking about school, teachers, and so on, and I asked, "If you were to tell me your teacher is nice, what would you mean by that?" She wasn't a quick-answer kid. She screwed up her face, half closed her eyes in thought, and kept me waiting a few seconds before replying. *"Nice.* Nice." She repeated the word, then said, "Well—I think I would mean that my teacher is comfortable to be with. That's what nice means." She sounded satisfied with her explanation.

I thought, *Yes. "Nice" is comfortable to be with, whatever the age or the relationship.*

How do we help people to be comfortable with us?

It's a big topic. I'm inclined to think that we do that best by just being ourselves and letting the other person be himself or herself. Accepting a person for what he is contributes largely to a feeling of comfortableness. Conversely, when we do not accept people as we find them but rather attempt to change them all the time, it comes across to them as "She

11

doesn't like me the way I am." It's difficult to feel comfortable in such a situation.

It's exciting to discover in the Bible (Ephesians 1:6) that *God accepted us* because of His beloved Son, Jesus Christ. And God accepted us just as we were. He didn't go about to change us first. I love the verse in Revelation 1:5 that says He loved us and washed us from our sins. In that order. Not washed and loved. He loved us first. He accepts us as we are. That just has to be "nice"; it certainly made me feel comfortable!

Perhaps a good way to sum up for us what "nice" entails would be to study the Golden Rule: *Whatsoever ye would that men should do to you, do ye even so to them.*

TODAY'S THOUGHT: I can cause someone to feel comfortable with me today.

HOW TO HAVE A BEST DAY

BIBLE READING: Psalm 118:23-29

"Have a good day," the store clerk said in a mechanical manner, as she bagged the groceries and handed them to Frances.

Gritting her teeth, Fran turned to a fellow customer and said, "I get *so* tired having just about everybody I meet tell me to have a good day."

Maybe you agree with disgruntled Fran.

So how about aiming for a best day, instead?

"How can I have a best when I never have a good day?" some will complain.

Personally, I've found a simple, workable formula. It's this: First thing in the morning, honestly turn your day over to God. I don't mean in a pious "leave it to the Lord" sense, a withdrawal from personal responsibility. I have in mind squarely facing up to the known realities as well as the unpredictables the day can bring, then talking it over with our loving Father, asking Him to supply each hour's needs. Another thing, *thanking the Lord ahead of time for what He is going to do,* then stepping out the door expecting Him to be all that He has promised to be, makes for the best kind of day. I like to add, "And Lord, because you are so good to me, will you please give me the privilege of being a special help to someone else today?"

That offering of yourself makes for an especially good day. When Jesus said it is more blessed to give than to receive, He was not just framing a noble sentence. The statement is loaded with implications that we have probably not even begun to fathom. But we can try. We can practice giving, and the finest gift is ourselves, our time given to help someone.

13

Maybe we have things all turned around, tending to think of a good day as one in which everything comes our way; few or no frustrations; much success—and of course those make for good feelings throughout the day. However, for the inner joy that makes the day stand out as "best," we need the fulfillment of our desire to give, to meet someone else's need.

Some of the emptiest people I know, Christians who have little joy in their faces and not much excitement in their daily lives, are occupied solely in meeting their own needs. And at the end of the day many of them are sighing, "Another day—and what has it brought me?"

It need not be so, for each day is "the day which the Lord hath made." By an act of the will, we can rejoice in it, whatever its hours bring; it can be a best day.

TODAY'S THOUGHT: Rejoicing by the minute makes possible rejoicing by the day.

WHAT CAN A MOTHER DO?

BIBLE READING: Genesis 6:17—7:1

What can a mother do?

The question is as old as motherhood itself. It may be that we can find some answers if we will look back over the centuries.

Mother Noah, perplexed by the problems of an age whose morals so closely paralleled the standards of our own era, must have asked herself, "What can a mother do?" Undoubtedly she had to listen often to the pre-Flood equivalent of, "What's the matter with you folk? Are you crazy or something? Old Noah trying to *save* everybody. Him and his ark and his gloomy predictions!" And what about the times when her boys would come home upset over all the scoffing? When they said, "Mom, can't you *do* something?"

Mrs. Noah might have rationalized like this: "Husband, we have to think of our sons. A boy shouldn't have to go around apologizing for his father's queer behavior and talk—even in the name of religion."

But she didn't. And when the promised judgment fell, her sons were safe in the shelter ordained by God for those who believed Noah's message.

The New Testament has its sampling of mothers who must likewise have questioned at times. The mother of James and John, for instance. Perhaps she had lived with the fond hope of seeing "Zebedee and Sons" on her husband's business establishment, instead of which her sons took themselves off to be disciples of an almost unknown—though coming—prophet, spelling death to their financial future and the family's expectations. She might have chided

15

them thus, "Think of the business your father has built up. And he did it all for you—"

The glimpse we are given of that mother would indicate the opposite. "Then came the mother of Zebedee's children with her sons, worshipping him, and desiring a certain thing of him" (Matthew 20:20).

Some have criticized her for that request. But she asked nothing but the best for her two sons, and what mother doesn't want that! And we should note that she came with them (she didn't send them); second, she had her priorities straight: she came *worshiping* Jesus, first, before making her request. And what a request! That her sons might be close to Him in His glory. What more can a mother ask?

We might look, too, at Timothy's mother and grandmother, Eunice and Lois. Their place in history was procured through their insistence on teaching a young lad the Scriptures which were able to make him "wise unto salvation" (2 Timothy 3:15). There must have been times when Timothy's Greek father opposed such teaching of his son.

There will always be conflict in raising a child for God in a God-dishonoring society. Situation ethics would require that we accommodate to the times in which we live. Nevertheless, when we sincerely ask of God, What can a mother do? the Lord will honor that request. He will help, and guide, and bless such a mother.

TODAY'S THOUGHT: There is always at least *one godly thing* a Christian mother can do.

WILL MY HUSBAND *EVER* BE SAVED?

BIBLE READING: 1 Peter 3:1-7

"I've prayed for Bill ever since I came to know the Lord," Alice lamented. "Sometimes I wonder if he will ever come to accept Christ as his Savior."

Many women find themselves in the same box as Alice. They have married while unsaved. Then with conversion to Christ came numerous changes. They were happy changes for the wife. But for the husband, when the conversion is not simultaneous, it's a different story. Often the man feels left out, robbed of the woman he married; their interests are totally different.

Frequently there are other problems inherent in the situation. For one thing, although the wife is now a believer in Christ, she hasn't become an instant saint. She has a long way to go toward spiritual maturity. The husband, meanwhile, will have unreasonably high standards for his Christian wife (the unsaved almost always have higher standards for us as Christians than we do for ourselves). Consequently, when the wife doesn't quite live up to his expectations—when she loses her temper, for instance, he may be quick to point out that flaw in her professed "new life in Christ."

But back to Alice's question regarding her husband's salvation. She can comfort herself that *because she is praying for him,* he is in a good position to be saved. Perhaps if she had not come to Christ, no one would ever have prayed for his salvation. Also, Alice has the consolation and assurance that God is interested in saving her husband: "He is not willing that any should perish" (2 Peter 3:9).

17

The Scripture portion for today emphasizes some things the saved wife can do herself that "her prayers be not hindered." Some unsaved husbands are very perceptive of how Christianity works in the believer's life. One man, himself unsaved, would prescribe for his wife when she became upset with something: "Go read your Bible; it seems to calm you." On one occasion when he made that suggestion, the Holy Spirit convicted her that she had not been spending much time in God's Word. She admitted that, after first asking her husband to forgive her for her short temper. That melted him to the point where she felt free to say, "It would be wonderful if we could read the Bible together." And he agreed. He was not immediately saved. But his willingness to go part way with her encouraged her to pray more, to believe more strongly that God was working in her husband's heart, and to pay attention to her own behavior and words before him. In time, her prayers were answered and now, together, the couple lives for God and enjoys fellowship with one another.

TODAY'S THOUGHT: Attitudes speak louder than words.

YOU *CAN* HAVE THE DESIRE OF YOUR HEART

BIBLE READING: Psalm 28:6-9

Some years ago a Scottish opera singer was persuaded to go to a gospel crusade to hear a converted opera singer. That night, Scotland's Charlotte Williams gave her heart to the Lord. For her it was simultaneously a giving of her talents in Christ's service. However, not long after, she fell prey to a throat infection that stopped her singing. Wholly committed to God, she went to her knees and prayed, "Lord, I'll do *anything* you want me to do—scrub floors—*anything;* just keep me close to you. Even though I never sing again, I love You with my whole heart."

She rose from her knees and reached for her Bible. Opening it at random her eyes lit on, "My heart greatly rejoiceth; and with my song will I praise him" (Psalm 28:7).

Comforted and inspired, Charlotte immediately wrote a hymn on the theme of praise, and through the years it has blessed thousands.

God knew that the desire of that woman's heart was to glorify Him. He could have used her in other ways. But He knew, too, that singing was her very life. He did not take away the desire of her heart. Now Charlotte Zarfas, she is still singing.

Sometimes we tend to think of God as a kind of killjoy, just waiting to find out what we enjoy so that He can snatch it from us. Yet the Scripture assures us of the very opposite. God is love—and love does not seek to obstruct us in our desires to serve the Lord. Rather we read in Psalm 37:4, "Delight thyself also in the Lord; and he shall give thee the desires of thine heart."

19

Are you thinking, *But I don't always get the desires of my heart?* Perhaps that causes you to doubt God and His love, at times.

If we could only know, we would possibly be eternally thankful to the Lord for not always giving us what our hearts desire.

Then, perhaps we need to take a look at what we have desired of the Lord. The practical James has this word for us in 4:3: "Ye ask and receive not, because ye ask amiss" (the wrong thing or with the wrong intent).

The sure way to obtain from God the desires of our hearts is to stay close to Him, to genuinely delight ourselves in the Lord. And He *will* give us the desires of our hearts. He said so in His Word.

TODAY'S THOUGHT: Delighting ourselves in the Lord means praising Him both *before* and *after* He grants our desires.

THE CONTAGION OF JOY

BIBLE READING: John 15:10-14

Some things are contagious and they're bad for us. We do everything in our power to avoid catching them. Then there are the good things—like joy.

I'm reminded of a neighbor who breezed in one morning and said, "I'm in a very happy frame of mind this morning. Just thought you'd like to know."

I did like to know. For by knowing, I could share her good feelings and add to my own happy frame of mind. She didn't linger to explain. She didn't have to. I greatly appreciated the fact that she believed my knowing she was happy would have meaning for me.

We don't always have to say it; sometimes the sparkle in our eyes speaks of our happy frame of mind. Pat made that Monday morning quite special for me. All day long I could see in my mind her smiling face.

Some people cannot tolerate another's obvious happiness. It's easier for them to weep with those who weep than to rejoice with the one who is rejoicing. God has made us all different, possibly in order that we can help meet each other's varying needs, but my own joy at Pat's overt cheerfulness made me realize afresh how important it is to rejoice with those who rejoice.

What is it that might keep us from being able to key in with another person's happiness? Is it perhaps that we have been programmed to expect less joy in our daily experience, as *Christians*? Yet, is not joy one of the primary blessings the Lord Jesus promised to us?

In a sense, joy is the hallmark of the Christian. It stamps us as being His and being a believer in His promises. "Ask,"

21

Jesus said, "that your joy might be full" (John 16:24). It's ours for the asking.

When our Lord wanted to teach a truth, He sometimes chose a child as an example. A child tends to believe, and Christ's promises are for believing. As His children we cannot only have joy ourselves, we also can pass it on. Possessing inner joy, we will be fitting witnesses of Christ's life in us, for real joy will not stay hidden; it will bubble over. Without even being aware of it at times, we will be passing on that good thing to those around us. That is the contagion of joy.

TODAY'S THOUGHT: Joy is as contagious as gloom and a hundred times more attractive.

GETTING ON WITH WHAT
WE KNOW

BIBLE READING: 2 Peter 1:1-8

One of the secrets of growth is learning and *doing*. We learn a little more, we do a little more, and we become something more. That is never more true than in the spiritual realm. Yet how often we excuse ourselves with, "If only I understood more," or, "The Bible is so hard to *understand*."

Peter tells in the verses we have read today that God has given us "all things that pertain to life and godliness"—all that we need to "live godly in Christ Jesus," as Paul phrased it (2 Timothy 3:12). Because we know that, maybe we need to pay heed to doing it.

We can thoroughly empathize with Mark Twain when he wrote, "It's not what I can't understand in the Bible that troubles me; it's what I do understand."

C. S. Lewis echoes that admission in *A Grief Observed:* "I know the two great commandments and I'd better get on with them."

It has always been a comfort to me, brought up as I was with practically no Bible emphasis, that early in my Christian life I found enough that I could understand in the Bible. It was then up to me to try with God's help to implement the knowledge.

Sometimes it's a "cop-out" when we excuse ourselves by saying, "I can't—I just don't know enough."

True. None of us knows as much as he would like to. But we *can* "add to our faith knowledge." Then from the new knowledge we can look into our responsibility as to how to best use what we've learned.

23

Perhaps the most common failure is in witnessing. We often rationalize that we don't know enough to be worthwhile witnesses.

One way to overcome that seemingly natural hesitancy to share the best of all good news is this: ask yourself, How much knowledge did it take to lead me to Christ? What impressed me to listen? What convinced me of my need to be saved? Thoughtful answers to those questions might cause you to feel that—yes—you are equipped with the knowledge to be a witness for Christ.

Sometimes I ponder what my life might have been had not a faithful Christian communicated his faith and his knowledge and pointed me to the Savior.

TODAY'S THOUGHT: God will use what you *do* know today.

WHAT MADE HER SO GREAT?

BIBLE READING: 2 Kings 4:8-10

We speak of her as "the Shunammite woman" because her home was in Shunem. The Bible calls her "a great woman." There's nothing to indicate why she had that title *before* the Elisha episode. But in taking a close look at her attitudes and actions in connection with the prophet, we find some great characteristics we could well emulate.

1. That unnamed women was *observant*. She saw beyond what was happening inside the four walls of her own home. Some of us don't always do that, then when someone nearby finds a need and meets it we say, "Now why didn't *I* think of that?" The Shunammite women observed the man passing her door.

2. She was *thoughtful of others*. Apparently she was not at first aware how important was the man she invited in for a slice of homemade bread. So she didn't "have an angle" in being generous.

3. She was *unselfish*. She didn't figure, I've just enough for my own family. Nor can we assume that she knew the widow's oil story (though it is in the same chapter). So she was not giving in order to see how much she might get in return.

4. She *showed a concern for God's servant*. At one point she recognized who Elisha was, or on one of his frequent visits, he likely told her. And that gave her another idea.

5. She *could put herself in another person's shoes*. Perhaps she said, "If I were this man of God, would I want to keep on going, or would I welcome a spot where I might rest in my comings and goings?"

6. She was a *self-starter*. Having pondered the need, she began to formulate a plan.

7. She obviously *consulted her husband.* Note that she told her idea to her husband before going any farther with it. "Let *us*—" She may have suggested, "Do you think it would be a good thing if we would provide shelter for the prophet?"

8. She was *sensible* and *realistic.* Her plans included enough and no more: a bed for rest, a table for refreshment or for work, a stool—for prayer? a candlestick to hold the light. No needless frills.

9. She *followed through.* Because she "kept it simple," her plan was achievable. Many times our ideas to help people are commendable, but they're so grandiose that we get bogged down and never implement them.

10. It all adds up to her being *given to hospitality.* The Bible exhorts you and me to be hospitable and offers exciting possibilities of reward (some have entertained angels! Hebrews 13:2). For the Shunammite woman it meant a place in history. For us, who knows? Obedience is often its own reward.

TODAY'S THOUGHT: What better day to start aiming to be great in God's sight?

HOW LOVE COVERS

BIBLE READING: 1 Corinthians 13:4-7; 1 Peter 4:8

Love covers a multitude of sins, the Bible assures us. But, like many others, I tend to skip once over lightly the verse that is familiar. I'm grateful, therefore, to a new friend who helped me to realize the practical outworking of this verse in everyday life.

She came to me and said forthrightly but without any note of hostility, "I feel put down by you." Nobody had ever said that to me before so I was naturally taken aback. However, from the little knowledge I had of the woman I respected her; I knew she must have a reason for what she'd just said.

"Tell me what you mean," I asked, adding, "That will help me to understand; then we can discuss it." I then tried the best I knew how to convey to her that the very last thing I would ever want to be guilty of was putting another person down.

As she explained from her point of view I began to see what she meant. Her grievance was, apparently, that I had added something to a piece of information she had given in a group conversation—and not just once. Maybe I'm too prone to do that. I travel and read a lot, and some of my friends tend to look to me for bits of information. That is not an excuse for me to put another person down, however. Nor would I consciously stoop to such tactics.

It was not the offense itself or my ready apology that spawned a real friendship between us from that time. It was her "caring enough to confront" as the psychologists call it. I see it as love covering by *un*covering. She might have kept quiet about what was irking her, meanwhile nursing a grudge against me (and no matter how much we nurse a grudge, it won't get better without honest treatment). Or, she could have drawn others into the matter with possible deplorable results. She did neither. I will always admire her for how she handled what could have been a sticky, touchy situation. It took courage, for she had no way of predicting my reaction. I might have bristled, denied any "putting down," and suggested she was slightly paranoid.

I learned a fine lesson. How thankful I am that the Lord worked in both of our hearts, keeping us sensitive in our interpersonal relationship. Most of all, I learned that love does cover even unrecognized sins and shortcomings.

TODAY'S THOUGHT: God always has someone around to teach us—if we will be teachable.

CASH IN THE BANK

Bible Reading: Psalm 23; Philippians 4:19

Ask any homemaker what is her most pressing daily problem. Many of them will reply, "Skyrocketing prices."

Inflation is a household word and no end is in sight.

I'm sure that, like me, you take down from the shelf an item that has been there for a few weeks and find the price mark significantly lower than the cost of replacing the can or packaged item. Many people are having to face up to the fact that they can no longer afford certain things they had taken for granted. We're all having to decide what we can get along without.

Such is the earthly scene: belt-tightening and more belt-tightening.

What if the economy of heaven were so unstable? What if it were subject to inflation? What if heaven's riches were dependent upon and fluctuated according to the Dow Jones averages? How much faith could we then place in the promissory note, "My God shall supply all your needs" (Philippians 4:19) or in, "The LORD is my shepherd; I shall not want" (Psalm 23:1)?

But—read Philippians 4:19 again. What is the supply "according to"? It is not according to our hopes, not according to our expectations, or our thinking or planning. It is *according to His (God's) riches in glory by Christ Jesus!*

We should note, also, that the promise is to meet our need, not our *greed.*

How great are God's riches in glory by Christ Jesus?

I don't know. But I do know that because God's Word says it, His resources are sufficient for all the needs of every individual who will ever, *in Jesus' name,* lay claim to them.

Thus, the oft-quoted promise (Philippians 4:19) can be likened to a blank check drawn on the account of the Lord Jesus Christ.

Think, what do you really need right now?

Next, figuratively "fill in the amount" (the need).

Then, present the check. With Jesus Christ as the guarantor, heaven's bank will honor your check. Not one of His checks has ever bounced.

We can know the truth of "I shall not want," when we have internalized by faith, "My God shall supply all your needs."

TODAY'S THOUGHT: A check has no value until it is cashed.

IT PAYS TO BE SIMPLE

BIBLE READING: Psalm 116:1-8

I would like to continue with yesterday's theme: cashing our Philippians 4:19 checks.

Mary Ann was excitedly telling her sister-in-law about an answer to prayer.

"How d'you know it wouldn't have happened anyway?" was the sister-in-law's wet-blanket response. "What makes you think your *prayers* had anything to do with it?"

"Guess I'm just simple enough to believe," Mary Ann answered with a warm smile. "The Lord has promised to supply my needs, and that was a need so I prayed. It's that simple."

Whether or not she was aware of it, Mary Ann was proving the verse, "The Lord preserveth the simple" (Psalm 116:6).

Some Christians are just too sophisticated for their own good. They are not, in a practical sense, *believers.*

What is it that prevents us from taking the Lord at His Word?

Is it sheer unbelief?

Is it our inability to comprehend that God delivers on His promises?

Is it that we have allowed others to impose their doubts upon us?

Is it a supposition that God's promises are for another era or dispensation; not for us today?

Whatever the reason, we rob ourselves when we do not take God at His word. Not to believe our heavenly Father is to be like a child who distrusts his parents' promises.

Being simple, in the sense in which Mary Ann meant it,

31

is not something to be despised. Rather she is exemplifying a childlike trust, which the Lord Jesus Christ commended. When He was looking around for a model of a subject in His kingdom, He set a child in their midst (Matthew 18: 2). A child's trust, unless it is violated, is generally pure and uncluttered with doubts.

It is no mark of foolishness, then, to believe our heavenly Father. How much anxiety we might spare ourselves by taking to heart the truth that "the Lord preserveth the simple," and being humble enough to slip into that category.

We would then have no problem about cashing in on Philippians 4:19.

TODAY'S THOUGHT: "Simply trusting" is letting God be God in my life.

THE TRUTH NEED NOT HURT

BIBLE READING: Job 6:24-30

Sandra, after the tragic loss of a child, had just ventured back into sociability. At a neighborhood Mother's Club meeting, a few of the women were talking with Sandra during a coffee time. For the most part they were comforting and sympathetic, but one said in a know-it-all tone of voice, "Well, there's always a reason for such things," and she began to enumerate some of the reasons, from her point of view.

That "Job's comforter" was little different from Eliphaz, Bildad and Zophar, all of whom presumed to know the why of Job's sufferings.

Have you sometimes been the victim of such a friend's tongue? Some problem arises in your life, some testing or trial comes—and before long you meet someone who "knows more than God" and who harangues as did Job's three friends?

What can we learn from Job in that situation? How did he handle it?

Job countered with, "Honest words are not painful" (Job 6:25). He was willing to listen if they could be objective and show him where and how he had erred. In effect he pled, "Don't judge me by my present talk. Don't you know that a desperate man cannot always be held accountable for what he says?"

In that day as in ours, the Golden Rule applies. Give to the person undergoing trial the consideration and compassion you would hope for in like circumstances.

We all know that God has various reasons for permitting the trials that life brings to each of us. They may be to refine us, or to chasten us. Ultimately His purpose is to mold us into the image of His son (James 1:12; Romans 8:29).

As members of the human race we are prey to trials. Life is not a television drama where, if we can only hold out till 9:00 P.M., every problem will be solved.

Not all of our trials will have happy resolutions. But it helps when those around us are understanding, rather than being diagnosticians who want to tell us the cause(s) from their superior knowledge of the ways of God. "He knows the way I take," Job concluded. It matters little what others think of the reason for our grief, sorrow, tribulations.

Joseph Bayly, speaking at a session on grief, stated: "Job's three friends could have gained immortality as the world's finest comforters if they had only kept their mouths shut."*

We can be genuine comforters who will be welcomed and whose understanding is appreciated. A silent squeeze of the hand is often more eloquent than any words we can think of. When we do speak, let's do it with empathy and love. People have enough to bear when sorrow comes, without having our added, "I know why."

TODAY'S THOUGHT: Knowing that God knows makes everything bearable.

---

*He was speaking at a Sunday school convention in Pasadena, November 1978.

34

PERMISSION GRANTED

BIBLE READING: 1 Corinthians 10:23, 31-33

I turned the dial of my radio just as a woman was saying, "So I want you to give me permission to do this."

The program was a talk show hosted by a woman psychologist. I listened for a little while and heard the psychologist give the caller permission. I didn't learn what she wanted permission to do, but I do know that I'm hearing and reading more all the time of the verbal sanctioning by one person of another's doing a certain thing.

Thinking it over, I began to wonder if some of the callers might not be just asking a stranger to condone something that their own consciences would not let them do without feeling uneasy. I know of some instances where permission has been granted for cheating on one's spouse. Another popular request for permission is responded to in these words: "If you feel like doing it, do it." In effect the person is being encouraged to believe that anything is OK if you feel like doing it, a "please yourself first" concept. No matter that it might hurt or inconvenience someone else.

Does this not savor of the defenses we used as children: "She made me do it," or, "She said it was all right"?

But we are no longer children. Moreover, the Lord has given us a mandate for our speech and behavior: "Whatsoever ye do in word or deed, do all in the name of the Lord Jesus" (Colossians 3:17).

That doesn't mean that we cannot discuss things, or seek wise counsel from a trusted Christian friend. But the true criterion as to whether it is right for us to do a particular thing is "Can I do (whatever it is) *in the name of the Lord Jesus?*" "Will it glorify Him?" "Is it in line with the Scrip-

35

tures?" "Do I have a clear conscience on the matter?" (I think it was Huckleberry Finn who said about his conscience, "It takes up more room than anything else in my insides.")

Without the peace of mind and heart that comes from being right with God, all the human "permissions" are not worth the words it takes to grant them. Indeed, such permission can be destructive to our peace. It will only be as good as the values and morals of the one granting it.

TODAY'S THOUGHT: God grants me permission to do everything that is ultimately best for me.

BUT WHAT ABOUT *MY* PROBLEM?

Bible Reading: 2 Corinthians 12:7-10

"Seems I'm forever helping somebody who has a problem. But what about my own?" Alice said to herself in the mirror.

You may have said or thought the same thing. No matter how engrossed we may become in other people, at the core we are self-interested. That's how we've been made, ever since the Fall. (We didn't see Adam trying to help Eve; he was looking out for himself.)

We have to come a long way in the Christian growth process before we can be satisfied with, "My grace is sufficient," when we're faced with a problem.

More than once I've heard a woman, frustrated and even a bit cynical, say, "That was all right for Paul. But what if he had had *my* problem!"

What was Paul's problem?

All we know is that it was physical; it was his "thorn in the flesh."

From other incidents we know that the apostle was not the kind who just accepted a situation when he could do something to better or to change it. So he sought relief for his problem. He asked God to remove it; he asked not just once but three times. We can't know why the Lord did not choose to answer the first time and heal Paul where he needed healing. Maybe God was testing Paul to see if the matter was really a problem, a hindrance to him in his work. On the third appeal, God spoke. And ever since Paul wrote his letter to the Corinthians we have been repeating the classic phrase, "My grace is sufficient" (2 Corinthians 12:9).

37

Sufficient for what? you might ask, quite reasonably.

And that makes me think of something my mind has toyed with for years. Much speculation has been voiced and written as to what precisely was Paul's thorn in the flesh. Some would be dogmatic, insisting it was an *eye* problam, and they submit their proof verses.

But we *don't know* the nature of Paul's problem. What if we did? Imagine what might well happen. Our argument could go like this:

"When God said, 'My grace is sufficient,' that was for *Paul's* condition. But my problem—it's far greater than Paul's ever was. How do I know that the grace God promised Paul is sufficient for what *I'm* going through?"

God knows us only too well. Was it not, then, in consideration for us and in His all-encompassing love, that He did not reveal what Paul prayed about three times and was given grace to bear?

We can take comfort, whatever the problem, that God's grace is not limited.

What is your problem? God's grace is sufficient.

TODAY'S THOUGHT: What I don't know *can* help me.

RESISTING THE TEMPTING
MORSELS

BIBLE READING: 1 Peter 3:8-12

Gladys is a fairly new Christian and has not had much familiarity with the Bible.

"I'm really impressed," she says, "with the practical way in which the Bible treats real life situations."

"Give me an example," I asked, intrigued with what she might have discovered in her reading.

"Well, look at this." She turned to Proverbs 18:8 in her Berkeley Version Bible: *"The words of a gossip are tempting morsels,"* she read aloud, then added, "That's so true!"

Gladys, like many of us, had learned from experience that friends and neighbors can be easily alienated as a result of gossip.

Why does the Bible take such a firm stand on the use of our tongue? James speaks of *bridling* it (James 1:26)— controlling the tongue, not letting it run away with us.

Not all gossip is with vicious intent. Some people pass along tidbits about other people for the sake of the temporary attention it brings themselves. But a little thought would convince us that such attention is not worth the price someone else may have to pay for it. Nor is it worth having that attention, because the very people who provide it probably do not respect the talebearer.

Gossiping is a game in which everyone loses. Yet how much sorrow and hurt have been caused by some who chase popularity and attempt to buy it with the currency of tattling. Thereby some people have been guilty of destroying another person's reputation.

It's good, then, to pray David's prayer: "Let the words of my mouth . . . be acceptable in Thy sight, O LORD" (Psalm 19:14). And it takes daily watchfulness to heed Psalm 34:13, "Keep thy tongue from evil, and thy lips from speaking guile."

Here is a simple preventative guideline. Before repeating anything about another person *who is not present,* ask yourself: Is it true? Is it any of my business? Am I being kind—Christlike—in telling it?

If the answer to any of those three questions is no, that should be sufficient for one to refrain from talking about the matter.

"A perverse man [woman] sows strife, and a whisperer separates familiar friends" (Proverbs 16:18).

You don't want to be guilty of that, do you?

TODAY'S THOUGHT: God created us with ten fingers and just one tongue.

(Tomorrow we will look at the other side of the gossip coin.)

IT TAKES TWO TO TATTLE

BIBLE READING: Proverbs 17:4-9

Every one of us has some weak point that Satan's darts can penetrate. With some, it's a too-quick temper; others have a mean or jealous streak, whereas for others the temptation to gossip is very hard to resist.

Whatever our problem or particularly vulnerable area, we all need help to be strong and to withstand temptation. The chronic gossip needs the help of someone who *will not listen.*

As our verses today make clear, it does take two to participate in talebearing. Verse 4 in the Berkeley Version says, "An evildoer listens to wicked lips, and a liar pays attention to a vicious tongue."

"But," you may be saying, "how can I stop someone from gossiping? I have no way of knowing what the person is about to say. It's not always possible to protest that I don't want to hear, or to be a part of any gossip."

That can certainly be a problem. And who among us wants to deliberately encourage one person to talk about another? However, there are some characteristic signs: a hand over the mouth generally signals, "I don't want anyone else to hear." An introductory, "I haven't told a soul," can also alert us to be on guard for possible talebearing.

What can we do when we suspect we are about to be the recipient of gossip?

Here is one proved step: ask, *nicely,* "Why are you telling me this?"

If there is no intent to tattle, your question will not create hostility.

On the other hand the malicious gossip is almost certain

41

to react with, "What do you *mean,* 'why am I telling you'?" And, predictably the gossip will become huffy and drop you from her list of listeners. A better result will follow if your frank question causes the person to do a little self-examining.

That, in turn, can lead to the person's giving up the destructive habit. She may even move into the positive area described in Proverbs 31:26, "She openeth her mouth with wisdom." No place there for gossip.

It needs to be said that not all confidence sharing is harmful. There is a commendable aspect such as when one person will alert another to a situation that calls for prayer. No need then to question, "Why are you telling me?" That sharing of confidence falls into the category of bearing one another's burdens. It is poles apart from the malice-motivated practice of tattling.

TODAY'S THOUGHT: There's a time to listen and a time to turn away.

OUT OF ORDER

BIBLE READING: Isaiah 30:15-18

Lynne glanced at the clock. *Good,* she said to herself. *I can just make it to the Laundromat and get my shopping done while I wait.*

It had been a hectic forenoon with one thing after another cutting into her time.

She stowed the laundry into the station wagon and headed for a nearby shopping center. Parked in front of the Laundromat, she grabbed the clothes and was just stepping toward the door when she spotted the sign, "CLOSED—machines temporarily out of order."

"That's *it,*" she said between clenched teeth. "I've had it. First the alarm didn't go off, next the toaster wouldn't work, then the washing machine flipped and overflowed all over the floor." She took a deep breath and spilled some more to herself. "Between getting ready for my in-laws' visit, trying to do a little work on my group Bible study lesson, and keeping the family happy, it's just *too* much. Now this!"

She shoved the bag of soiled clothes back into the car, then, seated behind the wheel, she sighed and almost gave way to tears. *Out of order. That's what I'd like to be right now. Then I could just rest, feel irresponsible, and let somebody else do all the things I should be doing.*

Perhaps you are empathizing with Lynne. Do you, too, sometimes feel you would like to put an out-of-order sign on yourself and just escape for a little while? I wouldn't be honest if I didn't admit that I have felt that more than once.

What would cause us to feel like escaping?

We might get some clues from what makes an appliance

get out of order: overuse—abuse—lack of attention that maintains it in order. The washing machine can't shout, "Hey, you're overloading me." It just quits. Your toaster can't complain, "The fuse is blown." It just doesn't toast the bread.

We are not inanimate, voiceless, mindless pieces of household equipment. Nevertheless we do get out of order, physically, mentally, and emotionally. So it's good not to have unrealistic expectations of our body's endurance.

The Lord who made us knows our potential for getting run down or for "blowing a fuse." For those who will appropriate it, He has provided the calming solution: "In quietness and in confidence shall be your strength" (Isaiah 30:15). As hymnwriter John Peterson expresses it, "There *is* a place of quiet rest."

Being quiet takes time and effort. "Study to be quiet," the Bible tells us (1 Thessalonians 4:11). It is in our quiet times that God can speak His peace to our hearts. He can show us the way to balance our lives so that we will not be inordinately pressured. When things pile up and the hours seem too few for the tasks, even five minutes alone with the Lord can help drain away the tension and produce a tranquil spirit.

TODAY'S THOUGHT: God can create order when we feel out of order.

MENDING THE FENCES

BIBLE READING: Matthew 5:21-24

It was the afternoon following the class business meeting and Marcia, the class secretary, announced to her friend Joan, "I volunteered you to plan our class social." When Joan didn't immediately respond, Marcia added, "Well, you weren't there last night—and I knew you wouldn't mind."

"What if I do mind?" Joan replied in measured tones that did nothing to conceal her anger. She turned and walked the other way on the street where they had just met one another.

The afternoon wore on and the more Joan let her mind dwell on the incident of the class social, the more miserable she felt. It was not the prospect of the time-consuming organizing and the subsequent work of the party for their large class that bothered her. No. It was her own sharp retort and leaving her friend standing on the street in dismay.

Joan knew enough to pray about her problems so she deliberately went to her bedroom to have a quiet time with the Lord. But that time it didn't work. It seemed as though a heavy curtain hung between her and God. She tried leafing through her Bible for some consolation, but even that did did little to remove the dismal mood that gripped her. Then to her mind came the words of the Lord Jesus in Matthew 5:24, "Leave there thy gift before the altar, and go thy way; first be reconciled to thy brother."

Joan learned that day what many of us learn in similar situations—that God loves us too well to let us be at peace when we have fractured some relationship. She did "leave her gift at the altar"; she did apologize.

"But," you may be saying, "Joan isn't the one who should

have done the apologizing. Her friend was in the wrong for presuming to thrust a responsibility upon Joan without first asking her."

It doesn't matter who is "wrong." To be sure, the other person's approach may be tactless or worse. Even so, you and I (and Joan) do not have to be reactors. Rather than allowing something to create a gulf between us and a friend, we need to speedily take whatever step is necessary to restore the relationship. Only so will we know the peace of God in our hearts.

I like it that our Lord had good expectations of His own people. "Go—be reconciled—come back."

So why should we let a day be clouded by the haunting feeling, *I've done or said something wrong?* If we have broken a fence—no matter what the circumstances—isn't it better to mend it as best we can? That is not primarily so that the other person will feel better (which should normally result). You and I will feel better for having been a fence mender, and we will know renewed fellowship with the Lord.

TODAY'S THOUGHT: The price of poor relationships is too high. We can't afford them.

MARRIAGE—SECOND TIME EFFORT

BIBLE READING: Ephesians 4:26-32

They were a middle-aged couple and had lost their first mates through death.

The scene was the new bride's dining room. Seated around the table with the newlyweds were a few old friends. I still recall the interchange between that couple on their wedding day.

The entrée was a large roasted chicken, and the bridegroom was performing his host duties, carving the fowl the best way he knew. His bride, watching him maneuver the bird and the carving knife, sniffed impatiently and said, "My first husband didn't carve that way."

I thought, *Oh, dear! What a start for a marriage! Comparing the first husband and the new one, to the latter's disadvantage—and before other people.*

It's a maxim that comparisons are odious. They are likewise devastating and humiliating to the one compared unfavorably. It's even worse when it happens in the presence of others.

How could the bride have been so insensitive? We had listened to the brief, to-the-point counsel of the minister as soon as he had heard their vows and pronounced them husband and wife. It was his custom to give to every couple this verse: "Be ye kind one to another, tenderhearted—forgiving one another . . ." (Ephesians 4:32).

But how soon we forget God's exhortation, as that woman had apparently done.

Predictably, the marriage was already in trouble. The

47

husband would no doubt feel that he had to defend himself, prove himself in a number of ways. That would keep him from being himself and from feeling comfortable in the new relationship.

The wife who so readily found fault with one area would likely be just as vocal about other flaws she would detect in his actions.

The attitude of *being kind* would have prevented such a poor beginning.

The *tender heart* looks for the good, rather than nit-picking for faults.

And a *spirit of forgiveness* keeps the channels clear between a couple, whatever their age, or the age of their marriage.

The beginning of a new marriage is above everything else a time for "forgetting those things which are behind" (even how the first husband carved the chicken).

TODAY'S THOUGHT: A new marriage is a time for new expectations.

WELCOME THE TWO BEARS

BIBLE READING: 1 Corinthians 13:7; Ephesians 4:2

Pam breezed into her neighbor Julie's apartment after their children were off to school.

"You're looking on top this morning, Pam," Julie remarked.

"Yes, that's how I feel, too. Both bears were working for me the last couple of hours."

"Bears! What are you talking about? Here, sit down. I'll pour us some coffee. Now clue me in about the bears," said Julie, settling into her chair.

"It's something our pastor talked about last Sunday," Pam began, "and I've been trying to practice it. It's about *bear* and *forbear*—he called them 'two bears,'" she explained. "He was telling us that love bears all things—in the sense of putting up with them, that is; and that we are to forbear one another—"

"Hey, that's worth thinking about," Julie said. "But what did you mean about these two bears working for you this morning?"

"Well, you know me, Julie. I get all worked up when the kids dawdle getting dressed, and when Jim doesn't take time to enjoy the good breakfast I've gotten up and prepared for him, and—oh, everything."

"Of course," Julie agreed, "but go on. What about this morning?"

"Oh, it's such a good feeling," continued Pam. "I asked the Lord to please help me especially to get the day started right for all of us. And you know, He did." Her face was radiant. "I didn't get all uptight, or impatient and a bit harsh as I often do."

"But wait a minute. Did the kids dawdle? Did Jim rush over the breakfast?" Julie asked, leaning over as though to catch the answer all the quicker.

"It was just like any other morning, actually. Except that I felt different, more loving and tolerant, so we didn't have any hassles. I just had to come over and share it all with you."

Over their coffee the two women discussed that new idea of bear and forbear as having practical impact on their everyday life. They especially expressed their thinking that it was forbearing *in love,* not passing an endurance test, the Lord has in mind for us. And they agreed that that calls for *momentary* grace to deal with frustration and pressures.

"I'm going to put out the welcome mat for these two bears at my house," Julie quipped as Pam left.

We would do well to put out the same welcome mat.

In our own strength we will have more failures than successes in dealing with daily stress on the biblical level of bear and forbear. However, God has promised to provide an unfailing supply of "sufficient" grace. We *can* know the good feeling that comes from triumphant obedience.

TODAY'S THOUGHT: God's Word never promises what is not available to us personally.

DEALING WITH THE CHILD
WHO LIES

BIBLE READING: Proverbs 6:16-19

Phyllis was at her wits' end. She and her husband had tried every approach they could think of to get their eight-year-old Jimmie to stop lying. She had even listened patiently when a neighbor suggested, "It must be something you're doing." And she added smugly, "My Paul never tells a lie."

Even if that statement were true, which is doubtful, it was neither kind nor comforting.

Lying has been with us from the beginning. The first recorded lie was uttered by the serpent to Eve in the Garden of Eden: "Thou shalt not surely die."

Because God hates "a lying tongue," we can never do too much to guard against lying ourselves, and we have a responsibility to make the truth important to children as they are growing up.

Why would a child habitually lie?

Sometimes fear is the reason. Take Jimmie, for instance: He disobeys his parents and rather than face the music, he denies having disobeyed. A family I know handled that serious problem in this way: when punishment for lying failed to stop the child lying, the parents talked, *without anger,* to the child, explaining the sinfulness of telling lies. Then they told him, "Jimmie, here is what we'll do. We will promise you that, *as long as you tell the truth, we will not punish you.*" Naturally, as Christian parents they also emphasized what is entailed in sinning, in confessing to God, and in true repentance.

No, the boy did not turn into a paragon of truth overnight. He still felt tempted to lie his way out of situations at times. But each time he came and admitted to some infraction, his parents kept faith with him. Much as, in the flesh, they might have wanted to administer punishment, much more did they want to help their son become a lover of truth.

Some children lie by way of exaggeration in order to gain attention. It may be that they learned that by listening to and observing adults trying to outdo each other and impress those around them.

Still other youngsters have heard too often, "You never tell the truth," "I can never believe you," or, "You're always lying," until they begin to feel, "What's the use? Mom and Dad will think I'm lying, anyway." Actually, such a chlid has hit on a very great truth that whatever our age we do well to heed. It's this: The person who tells lies forfeits the right to be believed when he *is* telling the truth.

"Lie not one to another," the Bible tells us (Colossians 3:9).

The finest teaching we can give our children and other young people with whom we come in contact is to be truthful at all time.

TODAY'S THOUGHT: Satan is the father of lies. But *we are not his children*!

WE CAN'T CHANGE EVERYBODY

BIBLE READING: 1 Corinthians 13:4-10

Martha frequently complained that other women did not seem to like her.

"What makes you think that?" a neighbor asked.

"Well—it's a *feeling* I get. It's not too easy to explain it."

"Maybe it's true; maybe it isn't," the neighbor, Sharon, responded. "I like you. Doesn't that count?" Then she added more casually, "Have you thought of any possible reason for someone not to like you?"

"Not really," Martha said, "although my husband has suggested that I have a tendency to want to change everybody."

"Hmm!" Sharon looked thoughtful then with a nod replied, "You may just have hit the nail on the head—or your husband may have, I mean."

Whether Martha's problem is real or imagined, it is all too common. There is in many of us a desire to change one thing or another in our friends or acquaintances as well as in our own family members.

Sometimes we can be genuinely helpful when we lovingly and graciously try to point out an area of behavior that could stand improvement. But few people are emotionally prepared to accept such suggestions. Usually the price is a deteriorating relationship. People do not take kindly to expressed disapproval, no matter how kindly it's intended. It all too often comes across to them as, I don't like you the way you are. Why don't you change? And it's hard for the person to think of the one making the suggestions as being kind and loving. Yet the Scripture bids us to be long-suffering and kind.

Moreover, the Lord made us all different by design, not by accident. How dull life would be if we were all carbons one of the other. It's the very difference in the individual that makes each person the unique "I" whom God created for His very special purpose (see Ephesians 2:10).

In a sense we are criticizing God's workmanship when we set out to change people (in the sense of making them more acceptable to ourselves).

There *is* a changing process that should interest every Christian. That is God-ordained change, with a positive, long-range goal in view. God has set before us a model by which to judge ourselves (not each other) and to set standards for change. Jesus Christ is that model. It is God's intent that "we all, with open face beholding as in a glass the glory of the Lord, are changed into the same image from glory to glory, even as by the Spirit of the Lord" (2 Corinthians 3:18).

Change? By all means: change in the right direction, toward the right goal, with the right motivation.

TODAY'S THOUGHT: When I am willing to change, it seems that others have changed.

I REALLY DON'T HAVE TIME

BIBLE READING: Ecclesiastes 3:1-8

"I'd love to, but I just don't have the time."

Wouldn't it be interesting to keep track of how often we hear that or say it ourselves?

Frequently it is a plain statement of fact; at other times it can be an excuse. When "I don't have the time" is the truth, then acting on it is simply being a good steward of a precious, nonrecoverable commodity. So we do well to question our use or abuse of time.

Especially in the home and with our children it's essential that we shun the excuse route. That doesn't mean we have to give account of our every minute. We do, however, need to be completely honest with a child. If, indeed, we do not at the moment have time to give attention to what the child wants us to do, there's nothing wrong with saying it. It's good to add, "But I'll make time a little later." A child can live with that without feeling Mom or Dad doesn't care about him. It's vital, though, to follow through and keep that promise.

Because we cannot "make" time, in order to keep faith with the child, we just have to let something else go.

Actually, it's been my observation that the boy and girl who can trust their parents to give them some time, are generally far less demanding. They tend to feel secure in their parents' love; they think, "I'm important. Mom and Dad like to spend time with me." Contrast the often-let-down youngster who continually hounds his parents with his whining, "You promised. You *promised.*"

Keeping a promise is its own reward in good relationships.

The wise use of time brings at the end of the day the sense that we have obeyed the scriptural injunction to "redeem the time," or, as the *Living Bible* paraphrases it (Ephesians 5:16), "We have made the most of every opportunity for doing good." It's a good feeling.

A sense of the worth of our own time will cause us to be sensitive and understanding of the person who on occasion has to say to us, "I'd love to, but I really don't have the time."

For our own part, a good test question is, "Can I offer that reason (or excuse) to God, and feel at peace?" If the answer is a clear no, we may have to do some reorganizing of our time.

TODAY'S THOUGHT: There are enough hours in the day for me to do what God requires of me.

HOW MUCH IS "SO LOVED"?

BIBLE READING: Romans 5:1-8

Janice was tucking the covers around her six-year-old Amy when the child asked, "Mommy, how much does Jesus love me?"

"Oh, lots and lots," her mother replied rather casually. Amy liked to use any delay tactic to keep from having to go to sleep, and that question sounded like one of her little ruses.

But it wasn't this time. Another such question convinced Janice that her little girl had something on her mind. "Why are you asking me about how much Jesus loves you?" she probed gently.

" 'Cause I was naughty today, Mommy."

"How naughty?"

"Oh, *real bad* naughty." Amy's eyes grew wide with a kind of fear as she persisted with her questioning. "How bad can a little girl be before Jesus stops loving her, Mommy?"

"Honey," Janice gathered her squirming daughter into her arms and assured her, "You can never do *anything so bad* that it will stop Jesus loving you. There. Does that make you feel better? The Bible says that God so loved—"

"How much is 'so loved'?" Amy interrupted her mother.

Screwing up her face in thought, Janice breathed a hasty silent prayer for wisdom, then soothed her small daughter with, " 'So loved' means enough to take care of whatever naughty thing you did today, dear."

But, conscious that her little daughter needed the comfort of feeling forgiven, the mother said, "Amy, why don't you just tell the Lord Jesus how sorry you are for being naughty and that you don't want to be naughty again. He'll forgive you. Let's just ask Him." Amy offered a brief prayer in childish words, then sighed, yawned, and wriggled a bit under the covers. Her eyelids drooped, and soon her even breathing indicated she was off to sleep.

Downstairs Janice and her husband talked over the bedtime incident. "Thank the Lord that she has a tender conscience, that she feels it when she has been disobedient and naughty," the father said.

"And thank the Lord that, although our child is too young to understand the words, He is able to save *to the uttermost* all that come unto him," the mother added.

There would be time and opportunity to teach Amy more about confession and repentance in the days ahead. But meantime she had grasped for herself the fact of sin, of displeasing God, and of how much Jesus loves her.

It's a wise mother who takes seriously the question of a child too troubled to go to sleep happily. And we have God's promise for the sometimes difficult questions that come from little lips, "If any of you lacks wisdom, let him ask of God" (James 1:5).

If we were to check, we might find that Amy's question had its roots in her hearing, "Jesus doesn't love you when you're naughty" (how often I've shaken my head as I've heard well-meaning mothers or grandmothers say that to a child). To be sure, God does not love anyone's *sin,* but He continues to love the sinner. That's what "so loved" is all about.

TODAY'S THOUGHT: God's grace can reach farther than we can sin.

58

I'VE SEEN—I'VE HEARD

BIBLE READING: Exodus 3:7-10

Every mother is familiar with the never-give-up wants and wishes of her children. Mary expresses her longing for a particular doll. Tommy daily hounds both his mother and dad for a bike. Later it will be for a car or a special trip. Whatever the thing desired, a child appears to believe there's merit in persisting. Sometimes we're driven to exclaim, "I *heard* you. I *know* what you want," and our tone says, "Now that's enough; I don't want to hear it one more time."

Isn't it comforting to know that God never wearies of our asking? It may take time for Him to grant our request because He knows what is best for us; His timing is perfect. But He has not forgotten.

It was a wonderful day for the Israelites, in bondage in Egypt, when God spoke from a burning bush in the desert of Midian. *"I have surely seen . . . I have heard . . . I know their sorrows."*

For centuries, at least some of the exiles had called on God for deliverance. Many times they must have been convinced that either God didn't hear their cry, was not aware of their plight, or—worse—that He didn't care enough to take action on their behalf.

It can be likewise comforting for us to know that "The Lord is not slack concerning His promises" (2 Peter 3:9). He will keep faith with us. He does see. He does hear. He does know. And He does move into the situation.

"I am come down to deliver them out . . . and to bring them up" (Exodus 3:8).

It would not have been enough—it would have been a worse fate than their present circumstances—if God had stopped at delivering His chosen people out of the slavery they were in. In His love and mercy He went far beyond, and in His time He brought them into the "good" land, the promised land.

We are not God. We can't always give our children what they ask. And it would not be best for them if we could. What we *can* do for them is point them to the only one who sees what they really need, who hears their cry, who understands their sorrows, and who can and will deliver them. And along the way He has promised, "No good thing will He withhold from them that walk uprightly" (Psalm 84: 11).

The greatest of all God's deliverance is that He delivers from the power and the penalty of sin, and brings us into the new relationship of being in His own family.

TODAY'S THOUGHT: If no one seems to see or hear or care, remember God does.

GETTING ALONG WITH EVERYBODY

BIBLE READING: Galatians 2:17-20

Should Christians expect to get along with everybody?

Do we have Scripture for or against such an expectation?

What about Romans 12:18: "If it be possible, as much as lieth in you, live peaceably with all men."

For too long I personally viewed that verse as the best of all excuses for not getting along with some people. "Aha," I would justify myself, "God knows some people are just too hard to get along with, and He has provided this 'out.'"

Then one day I took a new, hard look and let my mind dwell on a possibly different interpretation of the verse. I paused longer than formerly at, "as much as lieth in you."

What does lie in me? What lies within you, as a member of God's family?

The Bible has the answer. The very life of the Savior of the world lies within us, for "he that hath the Son hath life" (1 John 5:12). Is not "Christ in us" sufficient for us to deal amicably with other people? Are we not enabled by the Holy Spirit to make extra effort to foster good relationships?

As we allow the new nature to prevail over the old, we are often surprised at the practical turn it takes. That can be true in our new ability to live peaceably with everyone. Instead of arbitrarily "writing off" the person with whom we seem to have no rapport and whom we view as "impossible," the Christ-life in us helps to enable us to see the person as He sees that one.

We might also find ourselves asking, "What makes this

61

person not too likeable?" and, "What happened to make him/her this kind of person?"

Further, we will undoubtedly take a look at ourselves, and ask, "How hard am I to get along with? Are other people having to spend a lot of time praying for grace to put up with me?"

What lies in us will come out.

If it is selfishness, intolerance, unwillingness to reach out to others, jealousy or any other negative quality, the Holy Spirit is willing to help us pinpoint our own unlovely qualities and do something about them.

We can come to the place that Paul came to: what once was in him was crucified with Christ. And, like Paul, we can live with the assurance that "the life I now live . . . I live by the faith of the Son of God who loved me, and gave himself for me" (Galatians 2:20).

That is what can lie in us, and motivate us to live peaceably with all men.

TODAY'S THOUGHT: God was not giving us a cop-out but a *challenge.*

TIME FOR YOURSELF

BIBLE READING: Colossians 3:12-17

In our day there is much emphasis on leisure time. Industry endorses the four-day work week, which provides for many people plenty of time for themselves.

That new life-style has, in turn, spawned the phrase "discretionary time," time to do what we want.

However, for so many of us who were brought up in the Puritan work ethic mold, it's difficult to accept time for ourselves. We have to remind ourselves that it's not necessarily a cardinal virtue to work from dawn till dark.

Then, too, we may have heard quite often that a person can be judged by how she uses her leisure time (and the implication is that it had better be "something worthwhile").

We can learn from the Arab who just sat down one day—when he was asked what he was doing, his reply was, "I'm letting my soul catch up with my body." We need times to do nothing. In fact, our Lord set a pattern for us when He bade the disciples come apart awhile (with Him) and rest. They'd been busy together, meeting all kinds of human needs. Their work days had been long and pressured by crowds. The Lord Jesus understood the limitations of the human body ("He knoweth our frame", Psalm 103:14).

Probably no one needs to have that emphasized more than does the mother in the home. How can she stop to rest and do nothing, with every kind of household task staring her in the face?

Yet the time for herself is not a selfish concept. We all return to our duties much the better for having had some time off. The chance to walk away from pressure for even a short time helps us to gain a fresh perspective. It can restore our calm and revitalize us to be more effective.

"But when could *I* get away?" you might be asking.

There will likely never be a "right" time; nevertheless it is a good thing to do, for everyone concerned. So it will pay us to plan on taking some discretionary time, arrange it (we can usually accomplish what we set our minds to), then *enjoy* it.

The length of the free time is not so important as the fact of it. It's something to look forward to, to break the monotony or alleviate the grind. And it's important that *we feel no guilt*—no "policeman over our shoulder" sense of wrongdoing for having taken a break.

The Bible speaks of "pleasures for evermore" in the future (Psalm 16:11). We can feel sure that the Lord is not against either leisure or pleasure in moderation while we are here on earth.

TODAY'S THOUGHT: God has not called homemakers to be household martyrs.

WHEN LIFE SEEMS DREARY

BIBLE READING: 1 Corinthians 2:9-12

An elderly woman in a retirement home said, "It's the *sameness* that gets to me." She is a Christian not given to griping; she was explaining rather than complaining of her situation.

A young mother described her tedious days as "living in Dullsville."

And we all know the child who, becoming bored with his toys says, "There's nothing to do."

At every age there seems to be times when there's no relief from monotony—as though we were living in "Dullsville."

But does that have to be?

For the Christian who looks for it, every day holds its own brand of excitement. Oh, I don't mean Fourth of July, firecracker excitement, a momentary burst that then fizzles out. Rather, I have in mind the sheer wonder of being a part of God's exciting world, His plan. And if that were not enough, think of what the future holds for us!

"Eye hath not seen, nor ear heard—"

Nevertheless, the Scripture goes on to tell us that we need not be in the dark: "God hath revealed them unto us by his Spirit (1 Corinthians 2:10). He has drawn back the curtain of the future and shown us some of the glory that awaits us.

Let's ask, What have our eyes not seen?

The face of Jesus; the marks of the nails in His hands. Neither have we seen the place He has gone to prepare for us, or our loved ones safe and happy in His presence.

What have our ears not heard?

The physical voice of our risen Lord.

So much we have not seen or heard with our natural senses. But God has revealed *so much* to us.

It would be good, on the days when we might be tempted to murmur and complain about our dreary lot or our drab existence, to fix our minds on what we do have as believers. We do not have to wait until we reach the better land to enjoy some of its riches. Like Rebekah, we can appropriate them as we journey along to meet our heavenly Bridegroom.

It's a good testimony to the unsaved around us when we can be contented with such things as we have here and now. How often people scoff at what they view as our "pie in the sky" hope. We can help to refute that misconception. We can be satisfied and show it. God knows our needs for today and He has promised to supply them. With that daily assurance, and such hope for the future, how can life be dreary?

TODAY'S THOUGHT: We *can* be both heavenly minded and happy on earth.

SINGING IN THE MORNING

BIBLE READING: Ephesians 5:17-21

A dear friend of mine, Marjorie, frequently invites me to come and stay overnight with her. "I know how you enjoy the mountain view with your breakfast," she generally adds.

It is a soul-nourishing view, with nothing to block it or distract from it. When I can, I jump at the chance of such refreshment. But my friend has something else to offer to her overnight guest, something she was quite unaware of until I mentioned it. Marjorie is an up-in-the-morning lady, and I awaken to her lilting voice singing snatches of her favorite hymns.

What a beautiful way to start the day!

To be sure, we do not always feel like singing. I've been a bit cynical about the person who wrote, "I feel like singing all the time," but perhaps he did. That's rather high level for most of us, I think. But I do know the power to bless that comes from my friend's singing in the morning. And I've pondered as to whether I robbed my own family of some such blessing. The Bible does not use words idly, and we are exhorted to sing with grace unto the Lord. For those who don't feel like singing out loud, there's still no excuse. We are to make melody in our hearts.

Can you imagine yourself feeling and acting miserable while making melody in your heart unto the Lord?

It's worth noting that the singing is tied into thanksgiving. So, if you can't think of something to sing about, it will always be appropriate to sing, "Praise Him; praise Him," or "Thank You, Lord."

There's no more effective antidote to feeling down than

to "practice praise." Nor do we have to look far for something for which to be thankful. If we can get out of bed in the morning, if we can open our eyes on God's fresh new day, if we can stretch and take a deep breath and feel alive, we have plenty to sing about.

Starting the day with a song can set the pace for a wonderful day. The cliche "Have a good day" is not enough to guarantee anyone's having a good day. But we can program our own day to be pretty much what we want it to be. Singing along with your favorite Christian radio programs has a positive effect on moods.

And, just as my friend was unaware of how much her morning song blessed me, you and I can have similar influence on those with whom we share our mornings. We might even help to establish a happy mood for them, for the day. *Singing—as a mood regulator.* Now isn't that something worth thinking about? Is that, perhaps, something of what our Lord had in mind in the biblical injunction to sing and make melody in our hearts unto Him?

TODAY'S THOUGHT: We can't all be nightingales; but even sparrows sing.

WISDOM FROM A TEA BAG

BIBLE READING: Psalm 126

We never know where we will come across a snippet of workable wisdom.

A few days ago a friend came along and handed me a small octagonal tag with a little saying on it. "It's from a teabag," she explained. So, curious, I reached for a teabag, tore off the tag, and read, "A smile increases your face value."

I've long felt that to be a fact but I had not till then seen or heard it phrased so succinctly. A smile really does work wonders for the face. Here is a little test you might try: smile into a mirror. Now notice how the widening of the mouth, and stretching of the facial muscles are reflected in a new light in your eyes, a transformation of your appearance.

That is what smiling does for you, for you cannot help feeling better when you know you look better.

What about the effect on your husband, children, and friends?

Somehow, it would appear that for both Christian and non-Christian, the habitual expression is anything but smiling. Look at people on the street, in a bus or subway; in the department stores. I've observed even in church as I've seen the congregation from the choir loft. And I don't question that those in the pews see just as sad sights from their vantage point. Not too many are smiling.

"But," you may argue, "I don't read anything about smiling in the Bible."

I don't either. And some people declare categorically that Jesus never smiled. But I find that hard to accept. Think of how little children gathered around him! It would be hard to imagine a child's being eager to sit on the lap of a grim, tight-lipped, unsmiling Jesus.

The Bible does speak about *laughter,* and it would be a problem to laugh without smiling at least a little. The reaction of the exiles (Psalm 126) to their deliverance was first, "It's all a dream," then "their mouth was filled with laughter," and they told the heathen around them, "The Lord has done great things for us."

We, too, have been delivered from bondage. We have so much to rejoice in. Why then do so many of God's people go about looking as though He has forsaken them?

There's something appealing about a smile, whereas we are generally repelled by grimness.

A smile is something you can give away and yet keep. It doesn't cost anything, but as the little tag states, "A smile increases your face value." Since we can't usually see ourselves as others see us, if we don't want to be caught with an unsmiling face, maybe we should practice so that a smiling face will become our "everyday" face.

TODAY'S THOUGHT: A smile can be the shortest distance between two people.

YOUR RIGHT TO BE DIFFERENT

BIBLE READING: Romans 12:4-8

"They're as alike as peas in a pod," Frances said with a warm smile as she was introduced to her new neighbor's children.

But undoubtedly they were not all alike; alike in appearance perhaps, nevertheless they were two little individuals.

God has made us all different. We have different abilities and differing personalities to match our abilities. We tend to want to squeeze people into personality molds of our own making. We're not always willing to grant them the right to be different from what we are, or to do differently than we do.

Wise parents will make a point of trying to discern differences rather than concentrating on accentuating the similarities in their children. Such insight leads to a greater understanding of the individual child who is, after all, a unique person in his own right, not a "little somebody else."

Recognizing that fact, mothers will encourage each child along the line of his/her God-given abilities rather than making him a carbon copy of an older member of the family.

Sometimes, quite unwittingly, parents begin early to rob their boy or girl of their right to be different: giving the second child a name closely tied to that of the first or deliberately dressing children alike. The practice can militate against a child's right to an identity of his own.

There is in all of us a compulsion to be different. To be, as we say, "our own person." Some people have to almost fight for that God-given right.

When we are not willing to recognize that, while we are

all members of Christ's body, each Christian has different gifts, we may be guilty of encouraging some young person along a path that is not God's choice for him or her.

It's not that one believer is "better" than the other. God gives gifts and talents "severally as He will" (see 1 Corinthians 12:11). And because we are His workmanship, created in Christ Jesus unto good works, which He has foreordained (Ephesians 2:10), other Christians should let us use our particular abilities.

Usually, people do not tamper with another's life consciously, but we need to be on guard lest we forget that we are all God's originals. He does not deal in carbon copies, so we do well to appreciate the differences in each other, rather than attempting to produce sameness.

TODAY'S THOUGHT: Recognizing that God has made me one-of-a-kind, I want to allow for the created differences in others.

WHAT TO DO WITH YOUR DOUBTS

BIBLE READING: John 20:24-30

Nancy had been a Christian for just a few weeks. Saved out of a totally unchurched background, she was a radiant convert. Her new-found joy impressed even her skeptical friends. Then, alone one weekend, she found doubts creeping into her mind. *Is it all real, or am I enjoying a temporary fantasy?* She was tempted to throw it all away and go to her former crowd (who had given her a couple of months to "get her head straight again" and be back with them).

But God had not given up on Nancy just because she was about to give up on Him!

Later, she explained, "It would have been the most natural thing in the world for me to have gone back to my non-Christian friends. They would have welcomed me, I knew. But the Lord didn't let me go that route with my doubts. Rather, I went and sought out the woman who had first interested me in listening to the gospel. I threw down the New Testament she had given me and spouted, 'Here! I'm giving it all up.'"

How did the woman deal with Nancy and her doubts?

"She didn't react as I thought she would," Nancy related. "She set me down, made some tea, then said calmly, 'Do you want to talk about it?'"

In that free setting, Nancy spilled out her doubts, one of which had to do with the resurrection. "It seems to me that we don't have as much proof as the people in Bible times had. They really saw Jesus, heard Him speak, witnessed the miracles. And they heard *firsthand* about His death and resurrection. All we have is what other people wrote long ago. And it's not all that convincing now that I'm down out of the clouds."

The friend listened without interrupting or arguing until Nancy ran out of explanations for her doubts. Then she suggested some other aspects they might consider together. Concerning the resurrection she agreed that we have the reports of those who were eyewitnesses. But beyond that, we have the record of men and women who have gladly suffered persecution and—many of them—cruel death, for their faith in Christ. "Do you think they lived and died as they did just in memory of a *dear dead friend?*"

Nancy began to realize that her "well-thought-out arguments" were rather shallow in the light of the truth presented by the more mature Christian. She could see her doubts for what they were—Satan's attempts to destroy her faith.

She had, however, done the right thing with her doubts. She had brought them out into the open. And the light of truth had dispelled them.

God is not threatened with our times of doubting. It is He who gave us the ability to question, and He invites us to "come and reason together" (Isaiah 1:18).

TODAY'S THOUGHT: Strong faith can spring from honest doubt.

JUST DOING MY DUTY

BIBLE READING: Proverbs 31:27-31

There's something about the famous heroine of Proverbs 31 that irks many women. "She's *too much*," some of them say. "I could never live up to her standard, so why make the attempt?" others remark. Perhaps if we could question her, that multi-talented women would tell us, "I just did my duty." But "duty" is not the most popular word for many of us.

We might ask, "What is wrong with a sense of duty?"

Sometimes the only thing that gets us going on something is the knowledge that it's ours to do, it isn't somebody else's responsibility. For instance, some people are night persons. Morning is generally a "drag" to them, and it would be all too easy to do little or nothing the first few hours. But who is going to do what they're supposed to be doing? The dishes won't wash themselves; the house will not clean itself.

Doing our duty. Isn't this a matter of faithfulness?

Usually when one person shirks her duty, an added burden is placed on someone else. Perhaps it would be good for us to ask, How many people do I know who go through life doing only what they would *choose* to do?

A frequent excuse when we are faced with a duty we'd rather avoid is, "I'm not the type." Someone once said, "I get tired of the thinking that because we're 'not the type' we should always be excused. So what if I'm not the type? The work still has to be done, and if I don't do my duty I'm just making it difficult for other people."

The woman was right. If it's ours to do we had better get at it. Besides, there is great satisfaction in accomplishing something we would rather not do, but which is our duty.

Our Lord taught that if we are faithful in small things, we will likewise be faithful in more important areas (see Luke 16:10). No doubt that is a matter of cause and effect: doing the small duties makes it easier to tackle the bigger ones. And since every undertaking involves some duties, we might as well do them faithfully. Faithfulness on our part frees us from the nagging "I should have" that might otherwise plague us.

TODAY'S THOUGHT: It's in my power to be happy while just doing my duty.

IF I COULD ONLY FORGET

BIBLE READING: Matthew 6:9-15

Every time Clara and her friend Pauline met, the same subject came up: Clara reiterating what another woman had done to her.

"If I could only forget!" she would say, and would then go on to relate all the details of the injury she had suffered at the other person's hands.

Pauline had no desire to hear the story, yet she cared for her friend and didn't want to add to her problems by appearing unsympathetic. Nevertheless she knew that Clara needed to handle her feelings some other way, for her own good. So one day Pauline asked gently, "Do you really want to forget, Clara?"

"Yes, but I know I never can."

Right then Pauline remembered what her Sunday school teacher had said the previous week: "I am convinced that we can do almost anything if we *pray*, and *plan*, and *make up our minds*."

Clara was silent for a few seconds then she said thoughtfully, "I have prayed about this matter—maybe not enough, though. But I can't say I have ever planned to forget. And I know that I've never made up my mind to do it."

"How much does it mean to you?" Pauline asked, and Clara quickly responded, "Plenty. I'd give a lot to be able to forget the whole thing."

"Have you thought that maybe you can't forget because you have never *forgiven* the other woman? It seems to me that we have instant recall about other people's sins and faults. That is, until we can forgive them."

They parted. But Clara couldn't get the matter out of

79

her mind. She reached for her Bible, and, turning to the concordance, searched for "forgive." She then read a number of verses. One especially spoke to her: "Thou, Lord, art good, and ready to forgive" (Psalm 86:5).

"Am *I* ready to forgive?" she asked herself.

It didn't take much self-examining in the light of God's Word for Clara to see that her problem was one of not forgiving. And as she read the Lord's Prayer with new interest, her heart melted. "Forgive as you are forgiven" (Matthew 6:12) took on new meaning for her.

Some days later she met Pauline, who immediately noticed a new expression on her friend's face. "It worked; it *worked*!" Clara exclaimed. "I prayed, and planned and made up my mind to forgive *and forget* and oh, I feel so good inside!"

It's not easy to forget, even when we believe we have forgiven someone for a wrong. We are not God. We cannot do things in the measure that He does. But, even though we may at times recall a hurt or injury, we will remember without bitterness. The incident will not mar our fellowship with God. We do not have to go through life sighing, *If only I could forget.*

TODAY'S THOUGHT: With all the good things to remember, why dwell on the bad or the negative?

THE KEY TO GUIDANCE

BIBLE READING: Genesis 22:1-18

One of my favorite hymns has always been "I Will Guide Thee."

It's not just an inspirational lyric; it's a distinct promise from the Lord: "I will guide thee with mine eye" (Psalm 32:8). Such a practical promise, for who does not need guidance at some time; and who but God can knowledgeably guide us? For persons who have problems finding their way, a guide is so much more satisfactory than a map. I love it when someone will answer my plea for help with, "I'll show you; I've been there." That's a guide.

How can we latch on to God's guidance for our life?

The writer of Genesis 22 indicates a principle: obedience leads to further guidance.

God had commanded Abraham, and although it was the most extreme of commands, Abraham obeyed, without question. Tied into his obedience was trust that God would make it all come out right. Abraham was human, and he had not read the end of the chapter as we can today. Yet, it's significant that he said to his servants (22:5), "I and the lad will go yonder and worship, and come again to you."

We all know the story of his incredible obedience and trust.

God rewarded Abraham by revealing to him His plans for Abraham's future.

What can we learn from the patriarch's experience?

We have the clear-cut lesson that if we will trust God, He will trust us. He will whisper to us, by His Spirit, "This is the way; walk ye in it" (Isaiah 30:21).

We sing, "Trust and obey, for there's no other way."

81

How true!

The New Testament would add, "If we walk in the light . . . we have fellowship one with another" (God and His people). As we fellowship with Him He gives us guidance. As we study God's Word, He further guides us, but *only as we walk in the light of what He has already revealed.* Why should God give us further indication of His will for us, unless we are implicitly obeying what He has already made clear?

So obedience to God is born of trust in Him, and the two combined bring the guidance we need.

David the psalmist knew a lot about guidance; he was aware that God's guidance does not have a time limit. He guides not just until we're eighteen, or twenty-five. We will always need divine guidance, so it's good to have the assurance David had, "This God is our God forever and ever; He will be our guide even unto death" (Psalm 48:14).

Another blessing of God's guidance is that it will never confuse us. We can pray with confidence, "Lead me in a *plain path*" (Psalm 27:11).

TODAY'S THOUGHT: There is a guide who never falters, and where He leads I cannot stray.

SAFE FROM SEPARATION

BIBLE READING: Romans 8:35-39

Separation. It's an emotion-packed word, for usually it involves heartache. How vivid in my memory are the times when I've watched through my tears as a plane took off into the blue and aboard it our only daughter. True, she was heading for her chosen field of service, and we rejoiced that God was using her. Nevertheless, there are the long separations.

The Bible does not avoid such subjects. In what has been called "The Mt. Everest of the Epistles"—the eighth chapter of Romans—Paul spells out some glorious comfort concerning separation. As though throwing out a challenge to the past, present, and future, his words ring down through the centuries, *"Who shall separate us from the love of Christ?"*

Paul goes on to list the possibilities, beginning with physical suffering—and he was an expert, speaking from experience of persecution and trials. In a triumphant tone he dismisses those experiences, saying he more than conquered them. How can we be more than a conqueror over such difficulties? Paul says they *worked* for him (far from getting him down)! He called them "light afflictions" (2 Corinthians 4:17). In no way did they separate him from the love of Christ.

So much for the *past*.

It's the *present* we have to think of. But, according to the Scripture, nothing—no things—in the present have the power to separate us from the love of Christ. Circumstances may bend, may even at times break us. But they cannot separate us from our Lord or rob us of His love. "Having loved His own ... He loved them unto the end" (John 13:1).

What about the future?

Only the omniscient God knows what will come into our lives in the future, and from His total knowledge, He declares that no "things to come" shall separate us from the love of Christ.

Even our own *feelings* cannot separate us. We may at times feel that Christ is a million light-years away from us and we cannot seem to reach Him. Nevertheless we can be confident that no distance is great enough to separate us from Him. Satan would often tempt us to doubt (that's his chief strategy) and to feel all alone. But, as we read in 1 John 4:4, "Greater is He that is in you than he that is in the world."

No one and no thing can separate us from the love of Christ; we cannot even *separate ourselves* from Him!

TODAY'S THOUGHT: God's Word is more trustworthy than our feelings.

A TIP FOR THE COOK

One day as I was meditating on the well-known Romans 8:28, I said to myself, "This verse makes a lot of sense in the kitchen."

I read it again. "All things work together for good" and stopped and let my imagination take over. Suppose I were to collect all the ingredients for a cake and arrange them nicely on a cooking surface: flour, baking powder, shortening, raw eggs, salt, sugar—and vanilla for flavor. Then I call my family for dessert.

"Ugh!" I can hear the disgust in their voices as they turn from the unappetizing offering.

Foolish? Yes. But it points out a great truth.

Let's take the same uninviting ingredients and let them "work together," thoroughly mixed and baked in the prescribed heat, for the proved length of time to accomplish the best results. Now, open the oven door, allowing the aroma to penetrate the house—and you won't have to call anybody to come and taste!

Romans 8:28 would teach us that so it is in our lives. The individual "things" may not be such as we would desire. But, according to God's Word, let those things work together—better still, let God work in the circumstances as only He can—and the result will be better than we could have planned or hoped for.

It's when we insist on "doing it ourself," impatient and unwilling to wait for God to work on our behalf, that we suffer unfortunate consequences. We tend to act childishly, much like the little girl who, impatient to see the first cake or cookies she has baked all by herself, keeps opening the oven door.

The promise of things working for good is "to them that love God." In loving God we are also wholly trusting Him. We are confident enough to *believe that He is working* even though we may not see what is going on in our lives.

God knows the exact ingredients that must go into making you and me the persons He has designed us to be. He knows the "heat" we must endure and the times of waiting that try our soul. But He also promises that it will never be more than we can bear, (see 1 Corinthians 10:13), and God is faithful in keeping His word to us.

Job realized this divine principle in the midst of his tragic situation and wrote: "When He hath tried me [in the fire] I shall come forth as gold" (Job 23:10).

TODAY'S THOUGHT: God's oven is always at the right temperature to perfect His work in us.

WE MUST TELL JESUS

BIBLE READING: Matthew 14:6-12

We are living in a day when there appears to be great credence in the value of talking. "Talk it out," the psychologists counsel. "Don't keep your problems to yourself."

It's true, generally, that "a burden shared is a burden halved." But it depends on whom we talk to. It would be better to keep our mouths shut and never tell a soul, than to confide in the wrong person.

The disciples knew where to go and whom to tell when their hearts were aching.

John the Baptist was dead, cruelly beheaded by the king's command at the whim of a dancing girl.

For some of the disciples of Jesus that was especially difficult and tragic, for they had been *disciples of John,* the "desert prophet" until they had met Jesus on the banks of the Jordan and followed Him (see John 1:35-42). John the apostle and his brother Andrew had heard John the Baptist declare who Jesus is: "The Lamb of God which taketh away the sin of the world" (John 1:29).

Now they went to tell Jesus that John was dead. They could be sure of a sympathetic listener, one who could totally understand their thoughts and emotions, one who could speak the words of healing balm.

We, too, can go and tell Jesus when we are hurting, when we have emotional wounds that need binding up. When we go and tell Jesus, we are assured of an intercessor with the Father.

Because Jesus knows what is in our hearts and minds, He will never misinterpret our meaning or answer questions we are not asking.

When we take our problems to Jesus, we will never have to regret that we did, or wonder, *Should I have told about that?*

There are some things we cannot comfortably speak of to other people.

Peter had the right idea when he said, "Lord, to whom shall we go? thou hast the words of eternal life" (John 6:68).

Life brings to each of us its share of trials, and there will not always be someone around to whom we can go for comfort. But the Lord Jesus will always be there. It's never too late, never too early, never too hot, and never too cold; and we are never too far for His listening ear and understanding heart.

Elisha A. Hoffman spelled this out for our comfort in the hymn,

> I must tell Jesus all of my trials,
> I cannot bear these burdens alone;
> In my distress He kindly will help me,
> He ever loves and cares for His own.

BY LIFE AND BY LIP

BIBLE READING: Matthew 5:13-16

The neighborhood Bible study women were discussing ways in which they could let their light shine and, in so doing, glorify the Lord.

"Just by being *real*," a newcomer to the group suggested.

Asked, "What do you mean exactly," she found herself giving her own salvation experience.

"It was through a family next door who practiced what they preached," she explained. "We were not one bit interested in Christianity, but we were impressed—at least I was—with the consistency of that family. For instance, one evening a man came to our door. It was dinner time and Dad went to the door, listened to the man's pleas for help, then, feeling the man's tale was phony, but before shutting the door on him, Dad suggested, 'Go next door. They're religious. Maybe they will help you since that's in their line.' The man went and was invited into the neighbors' home. I learned that they gave him dinner and money for his immediate needs before driving him to a bus depot he wanted to go to. That was just one of the 'good works'; there were others. So when one Sunday the neighbors invited me to go along to church with them, I accepted. That was the beginning and not long after, I accepted the Lord as my Savior. I might never have done so but for people who were willing to let their light shine."

It's true that we are living in different days than when we could confidently and comfortably invite a stranger into our home. But were there not thieves and robbers in Christ's day, and strangers to entertain? Our Lord taught us the blessed consequence of reaching out to help the needy, and, the reverse, "Inasmuch as ye have done it not to the least of these, my brethren, ye have done it not unto me."

We would not knowingly turn the Lord away from our door.

The lesson He would teach us is obviously that He may come to our door in many forms and that it will always be right to give a cup of cold water in His name. We are the salt of the earth; Jesus said so. We are the light of the world. We can share the "salt," and we can spread the light. In innumerable ways each day we can evidence that we are His people by doing what He would do. In fact, when we are in doubt as to how to proceed it's always wise to ask What would *Jesus* do in this circumstance?

TODAY'S THOUGHT: You can't know who is watching your life today, but you can be sure someone is.

BLESSED ARE THE HOSPITABLE

BIBLE READING: Genesis 18:1-8

Six-year-old Cindy tripped into the dining room, a wide smile on her face. Right behind her was a missionary who, because there was no spare room, had shared Cindy's room. "Know what, Mommy and Daddy," the child said eagerly, "I 'cepted Jesus as my Savior last night. Miss Brown helped me. Now I'm going to heaven when I die." She looked delightfully satisfied.

Here is a beautiful instance of Christian hospitality paying off. The missionary guest was God's instrument for leading the daughter of the home to Christ while she had her life ahead of her to serve Him.

Like Shakespeare's "quality of mercy," hospitality blesses both the giver and receiver. In the first place, since hospitality is a distinctive of the believer (Romans 12:13), adherence to it just naturally brings God's blessing. It makes for happiness to sit around the table and share the good things God has provided. It's a way of saying "Thank You" to the Lord.

Then, too, there is always the exciting possibility of entertaining an "angel" (see Hebrews 13:2). The very one we fail to invite home may be our only chance for a unique blessing God wants to give us.

Think of the day Abraham invited the three guests to stay for dinner. Sarah might have said, "But Abraham, I'm too busy," or, "It's too hot to cook veal cutlets and make fresh bread." She didn't. And the Bible records that they *entertained angels unaware.*

Sometimes we can make friends for life just by inviting people home for Sunday dinner.

91

What, we might ask, would prevent a Christian from *wanting* to be hospitable (that is, people whose health and circumstances are equal to entertaining others)?

Some of the explanations (excuses, perhaps?) are:

"Our home is too small," or, "I have such old furniture."

"It's been so long since I entertained."

"I'm the world's worst cook."

"I never know how to talk to strangers."

Then there are those who rationalize, "If I invite the guest speaker to dinner, I won't be able to go and enjoy the meeting."

Not all hospitality involves either overnight accommodation or a meal. For example, once in a while you might get a phone call from a busy friend who says, "I have lots of people to talk to, but tonight I just need a *friend*. Can I come over?" You may just talk or play Scrabble. It's an opportunity for that friend to be herself and relax.

TODAY'S THOUGHT: One person's hospitality can dispel another's loneliness.

SEASONING CRITICISM WITH LOVE

Bible Reading: Matthew 7:1-5

Wearing a brand new dress, Joan met her friends Anne and Mary for lunch. Anne eyed the dress approvingly. Mary stepped back, scrutinized it then said, "Why *ever* did you buy *that* dress? Where's your taste, Joan?"

Later that day, in a department store Joan observed as a young woman met an older one—her mother, Joan supposed. After a greeting the younger one said in a warm tone, "Here. Let me fix that strand of hair." She did, then said. "There. Now you're beautiful."

Still smarting from her experience, Joan said to herself, *Why couldn't Mary have been kind like that young woman? Why did she have to criticize me so?*

What was the essential difference in the two approaches?

Love—and the lack of it. If we want to comment on another's clothes or appearance, there's a way to do it. "Speak the truth in love" (see Ephesians 4:15).

Criticism unkindly worded can be devastating to the one so criticized. It can cause the person to doubt herself ("Is my taste all that bad?").

Lovingly fixing the stray strand of hair could be calculated to make the older woman have pleasant memories of the incident. The mother might even have decided to be more particular before going out—who knows? But what if she had heard, "Your hair is *awful;* you look terrible"?

It's a fact that usually when we are criticized we don't hear, "Your *dress,* or your *hair*" (or whatever is being attacked; we hear, "You"—"You are—" and we feel wounded all over.

There is a sense in which a critic can make or break a person.

On the happier side, genuine criticism offered in an acceptable manner can often help us see ourselves as others see us and cause us to change for the better. The mature person can accept constructive criticism, not construing it as a personal attack.

It's the destructive kind that hurts; it shoots a person down. It can dull the edge of whatever ability one has through its power to destroy self-esteem.

We do well to examine our *motive* in offering criticism. Much of the "it's for your own good" variety is not that at all and had best be left unsaid. If we would honestly seek to master the art of acceptable criticism, we need look no farther than the Golden Rule (Matthew 7:12).

If you feel you must offer some statement, think of this: *Is my motive worthy and for the other person's good—do I know her well enough to feel sure she will not misconstrue my words as hurtful to her?* If so, go ahead—but season your criticism with the love that will take out any sting of bitterness.

We need to be supersensitive as to how what we say will affect the person.

TODAY'S THOUGHT: The right words "fitly spoken" are the best "criticism."

SO WHAT'S NEW?

BIBLE READING: Psalm 40:1-3

Some questions we ask each other are purely rhetorical. "How are you?" we say, not really inquiring after the other's welfare.

Another such question is, "What's new?" and again we are not generally interested in receiving a reply.

For us who belong to the Lord there are a number of valid responses to "What's new?" We know of things that are newer than tomorrow's newspaper.

Let's think of some of them.

For a start, what about *God's mercies?* Those are "new every morning" the Bible tells us (Lamentations 3:23). Think of it—just when we might be tempted to feel we had used up the mercies of God to us, we can revel in the truth that there are more where they came from, that tomorrow will bring a whole new set of God's mercies.

And maybe you are tired of the same old song? Well, the Lord is willing to do for you what He did for David the psalmist. "He hath put a new song in my mouth" (Psalm 40:3). It was a song of praise, and it became a medium for witnessing as others heard it. It's very interesting to read, "Many shall see it"! How can we *see* a song? Doesn't that say to us that, with the new song the Lord puts in our mouth, there is a corresponding change in our appearance and attitude?

Among the mercies which are new every morning are a new heart and a new spirit (Ezekiel 36:26). In the spiritual sense, God gives us a new heart *once* when we receive Jesus Christ as our personal Lord and Savior. Then, as we live out our days, how many are the times we feel and perhaps say,

"I just don't have the heart for (whatever it is)." It's at such times that God will encourage us to do what He has for us to do. He will, if we let Him, give us the right spirit to do what the day requires of us.

So—what is new?

In his day Solomon wrote, "There is no new thing under the sun" (Ecclesiastes 1:9). However God says, "I will do a new thing . . . shall ye not know it?" (Isaiah 43:19).

When God does a new thing for you and me, we will know it. And when someone asks us, "What's new?" we will have an answer (and it won't be some bleak and gloomy item from the newspaper). Every day of every month of every year of our lives we can be assured that God's mercies are new every morning. Great is His faithfulness.

TODAY'S THOUGHT: What if I answer, "What's new?" with *"God's mercies* are new today"?

APTITUDE—OR ATTITUDE

BIBLE READING: 1 Corinthians 14:33, 40

"I'm a slob; I know it," Jane admitted to her friend Carol. But the somewhat flippant admission did not hide a wistful note in Jane's voice. Nor did she look happy as she said what she did about herself.

"You're the one saying it, Jane," Carol responded and waited for her friend to elaborate on the state of her untidy living room.

As though to defend the condition of her home—and herself for permitting it—Jane said, "It's just the way I am. Now my *mom*"—she rolled her eyes—"my mom was the very opposite. You've heard about cleanliness being next to godliness. Well, to my mother *nothing* was above cleanliness. She was a nut about even one speck of dust. In our home there wasn't a thing out of place—and there wasn't much fun."

Carol listened patiently, then broke in with, "You know, fun and order *can* go together. I believe what you're telling me about your mother—lots of women are driven perfectionists. But should you let her attitude influence you for the rest of your life? You don't seem too happy living in an disorderly situation. Even with your God Bless Our Home motto on the wall."

"Oh, but I have just no aptitude for housework. I always hated it," Jane countered.

"What about now that you are a Christian? Maybe you'd like to forget all that other stuff and consider what the Bible says here. Look," and Carol pointed out the word "*confusion*." "Does that say anything to you?" she urged.

"Hm. Let me read that." Jane repeated, "God is not the

author of confusion but of peace." She had a faraway look
look in her eyes as she echoed, "Peace." Then, as the thought
occurred to her she blurted out, "If God is for peace and
order and all that, and I'm not, then I'm not really on His
side at all, am I?"

Already with the entrance of God's Word had come dis-
satisfaction with her present way of life.

Carol, the more mature Christian, pointed out that God is
not upset with the state of her living room. He *is* interested
in our change of attitude when our behavior is not becoming to one who names His name. Not only so, but the Lord
by His Spirit enables us to be transformed by the renew-
ing of our mind. With the mind thus renewed, our attitudes can change. We find that we can make a start at things
for which we seem to have no aptitude.

The Bible is of all books most practical. Its truth can
transform both our hearts and our homes.

TODAY'S THOUGHT: Where confusion reigns, God Bless
 Our Home looks strangely out of place.

WHEN YOU'RE FEELING LONELY

BIBLE READING: Mark 14:32-41

Loneliness. It has been called the disease of our age.

Similarly, we hear some people say, "Why should a *Christian* ever feel lonely?" And the tone often indicates that is not a spiritual way to feel.

I can't accept that concept, for did not God give us our feelings? To deny negative feelings is neither honoring to God nor helpful to ourselves.

Our Lord Himself, while here on earth, knew the pangs of loneliness. He did not deny them. Was ever a more poignant question uttered than, "*Could you not watch with me one hour?*" (Matthew 26:40 adds "with me".)

Pain research has shown that it's possible for human beings to tolerate higher levels of pain when another person is present. That explains why loneliness (unless we are alone by choice) is almost *in*tolerable to some people. In Gethsemane our Lord found not even one of His disciples who cared enough to stay awake. Not many hours later He would feel the ultimate aloneness, when from the cross He would cry, "*My God, My God, why hast Thou forsaken me?*" (Matthew 27:46).

No one but Christ, in all of history, could have *in truth* voiced that despair.

Paul, nearing the end of his life, wrote from his Roman prison, "No man stood with me, but all men forsook me. . . . *Nothwithstanding, the Lord stood with me and strengthened me*" (2 Timothy 4:16-17).

What the Lord did for Paul, He will do for you and me when we feel forsaken and alone.

The last few years have produced a spate of books on

loneliness and how to cope with it. **Many** of them have value; some have not.

Certainly sitting still and nursing feelings of loneliness will only lead to depression. We're living in what has been called "an alienated society" where neighbors are strangers to each other. And someone has to make the first move toward neighborliness. As Christians we should naturally have an interest in helping another person. Nevertheless, it's not always easy. So "reaching out"—a much-recommended procedure to end loneliness—is not the answer for everybody. Neither is the suggested gregariousness—getting into some groups—the solution for all lonely persons.

The one unfailing panacea for the lonely is clinging to the words of our Lord, *"I will never leave you nor forsake you"* (Hebrews 13:5).

A genuine appropriating of that truth will provide encouragement, hope, and the ability to face each day.

TODAY'S THOUGHT: Loneliness does not make me less of a person than if I were surrounded by friends.

MAJORING ON WHAT MATTERS

BIBLE READING: Romans 14:1-8

As the time approached for the family reunion, Sarah was torn by conflicting emotions. It would be so good to have all the family together, see the new babies, and meet a new bride who had joined the "clan" since last they all met. *But,* Sarah mused, *there'll be Aunt Freda—and wherever she is, there is sure to be arguing. She'll have some Bible-verse bone to pick to spoil things.*

You've probably met such people. They are never happy unless they are pursuing some argument. It might be a theological point on which the individual feels he has a private interpretation and about which he will neither give an inch nor will he let the matter drop. Generally, that mars fellowship, no matter how right the self-styled authority may be.

Frequently the arguing is over something that is totally nonedifying to all present, and the attitude of the one who starts it is no example of godliness. I'm reminded of Thomas a Kempis's words, "What advantage is it to dispute profoundly about the doctrine of the Trinity, if by your lack of humility you are all the while displeasing the Trinity?"

Paul must have run into some saints like that, who occasioned his writing his exhortation concerning doubtful disputations.

In Paul's day, many converts had come from other religions where customs were different. That is still true in many mission countries. And because, to a degree unknown in Christian countries, religion governs practically every phase of life, converts have to be taught new patterns of thinking about some practical, everyday matters. For example, "eating meat offered to idols" is still an issue at certain times of the year in Bangladesh. There, many ethical questions arise when a person turns from idols to serve the living and true God.

The essence of Paul's concern was that stronger believers should *receive* those weaker (new converts) since *God had received them.*

How often we are guilty of judging and misjudging! Yet it is on one basis alone that God receives us: "Believe on the Lord Jesus Christ and thou shalt be saved"; "by grace are ye saved through faith, and that not of yourselves: it is the gift of God: not of works, lest any man should boast" (Acts 16:31; Ephesians 2:8-9).

We all come in through the same door (the Lord Jesus Himself). New believers will all the sooner drop their old ways when we who are older in the faith lovingly receive them and *by example* teach them.

TODAY'S THOUGHT: What helped me most as a new Christian, and how can I best help a weaker Christian?

A TIME TO BE ASSERTIVE

BIBLE READING: 1 Peter 5:1-6

Pam and Katie were on their way home from a session on assertion training, which a friend had urged them to attend.

"I'm not sure," questioned Pam, "that this kind of thing is for me. Unless there's another aspect that I don't know about yet, the whole thing seems to be on a collision course with the Scriptures."

"Well," agreed Katie, "I'm not as good as you with words; but I feel the same. I just can't see myself demanding my rights and being manipulative."

"It's not that I'm advocating that we be doormats, letting everybody walk over us. That's not very honoring to the Lord," Pam continued, "But there needs to be a balance between self-assertion and 'in honor preferring one another.'"

What about the current trend?

How can we reconcile its teaching with God's Word, which exhorts, "Humble yourself under the mighty hand of God, that He may exalt you in due time"? Or Matthew 23:12, "Whosoever shall exalt himself shall be abased; and he that shall humble himself shall be exalted"?

Is there a time to assert oneself? I believe there is, but not for the reason we are hearing in some psychological circles today. Not that we might get our own way regardless of the feelings of other people. And not that we might "feel like somebody." As God's people we have many advantages. Chosen, redeemed, and on our way to an eternal heaven with Jesus, we can afford to be humble and thoughtful of others' rights.

To be sure, Paul on one occasion asserted his rights as

a Roman citizen (Acts 22:28). In so doing, he not only saved himself from cruel handling, but he also probably saved the men who would have administered the scourging from serious charges.

Concepts change, and behavior modification that is advocated today may be frowned on tomorrow as being altogether worthless or even harmful. The Bible—our manual for behavior—never changes.

Our pattern is our Lord Himself, who "made himself of no reputation . . . took upon Him the form of a servant . . . he humbled himself. . . . Wherefore God also hath highly exalted him" (Philippians 2:7-9).

The self-asserters would have us demand our rights.

The Christian who is following her Lord is happy to surrender her rights to Him. It will always be the right time to take a firm stand for what we believe, and we can do that in a gentle manner.

TODAY'S THOUGHT: It will always be right to assert that *Jesus is Lord.*

THE LITTLE LOST ONE

BIBLE READING: Luke 15:1-7

We were driving through the rich farm land of Ontario, taking our son to a youth camp. At one point it occurred to us that we had not seen a single person mile after mile. The equipment was out in the fields—but never a laborer. We began to comment on that oddity: big, prosperous-looking farm homes dotted the scenery, but there was a complete absence of humanity.

Suddenly we turned a bend in the road and an equally amazing sight met our eyes. As far as we could see, there were cars and farm trucks and tractors, parked bumper to bumper, wherever there was a spot and on both sides of the country road.

Our curiosity aroused, we could find no person to satisfy it. Speculating as to what was going on, we concluded it must be an important auction in the neighborhood. What else would inveigle busy farmers during harvest time and on a perfect day for ingathering?

Two days later we learned through a local newspaper just what had been happening. A three-year-old tot had wandered from his home and couldn't be found. Soon the telephone was buzzing with the heart-tugging story. And at that moment, nothing else mattered but that the little boy be speedily found and returned to his anxious parents.

According to the newspaper it was no random search. Every ablebodied person in the entire community had joined forces; they had literally—and systematically—combed field after field, marching the length and breadth of each, hand in hand that not one foot of land be missed, until the glad cry

105

echoed throughout the entire community, "We've found him! He's safe!"

I have never since read the Luke account of the lost sheep and have never listened to "The Ninety and Nine" sung without recalling that incident in Ontario on a sunny summer day.

"How far," I've wondered, "would they have gone?"

And I knew the answer was: as far as they needed to go to find the lost child.

19—More Salt in My Kitchen

How long would they have left the machinery standing idle in the fields and the ripe fruit unpicked in the orchard? As long as it took to seek and to possibly save from harm one little child.

That is what our Lord did for us. The Son of Man came into the world (out of the ivory palaces) to seek and to save that which was lost. He would never have been satisfied until He had fulfilled *to the letter* all that it took (His life's blood) to save you and me.

TODAY'S THOUGHT: What will I give up, how far will *I* go, to save one spiritually lost child this very day?

ONE WAY TO FEEL GOOD ABOUT YOURSELF

BIBLE READING: Philippians 1:16-21

Have you looked back over a day and thought, *What have I really accomplished today?* and your mind recalled some of the things you had hoped to complete?

Usually, at such times, we are a bundle of mixed regrets and a degree of disgust with ourselves.

What makes the difference between a satisfactory day and one that causes you to think less of yourself?

A key ingredient is having goals.

Goal setting is quite in keeping with the Scriptures; a classic example is Paul's "For to me to live is Christ" (Philippians 1:21). That was his long-range goal. In order to implement it he had a constant short-range objective. He "pressed toward the mark." That had top priority: "This one thing I do," he stated (Philippians 3:13-14). We can imagine him at the end of the day checking his progress.

It's my belief, and it is borne out in biographies, that the men and women whom God has used had known, defined objectives.

Sometimes setting goals is the only thing that keeps us going or even gets us started on certain projects. That is particularly true of the distasteful aspects of homemaking (we each have our own least-favorite tasks). Noting those on our to-do-today list of activities, then being able to check each off as done, will give us a good feeling about ourselves.

The snare to guard against in goal-setting is being unrealistic, biting off more than we can chew. For instance, Jane was aware that her dresser drawers were a hodge-podge, and that bothered her a great deal. So, one morning she said, "This is the day. These drawers are going to be tended to, every one of them." She started by dumping them out onto the bedspread. But before long she had to leave that project for a more immediate need, and she didn't get back to it all day. So she stuffed the contents back into the drawers, sighing, *I knew I shouldn't have attempted this,* and her face mirrored her disgust at herself.

Was the problem that she attempted a worthwhile task? No. The trouble was that she didn't tackle it *a drawer at a time,* a reasonable expectation of a busy wife and mother. The same principle would apply in any type of goal setting. It must be *achievable,* or we tend to feel we are failures.

Also, like Paul, we do well to consider, *Do my daily objectives contribute to my reaching my lifetime goal?*

It's important to remind ourselves that God will not like us less just because we can't always check off a thing as "done." But we will, generally, think less of ourselves. So goals should not be thoughtlessly arrived at.

TODAY'S THOUGHT: Setting goals helps keep us on course as to what *not* to do with our precious time.

I BELIEVE—I THINK

BIBLE READING: Mark 9:20-24

It was the second day of a women's retreat at which I was the speaker. During a coffee break I was alerted that one of the younger women was very unhappy. Not knowing any more than that about the situation, I prayed for special guidance, and later learned how the faithful Holy Spirit had worked. The young woman had voiced her feelings of disharmony with the group to a couple of roommates, adding, "I'd surely like to talk with that speaker, but I'm too shy. I'd never dare." But—and here was the working of the Spirit—those two were dear friends of mine from our very first congregation. "Oh, we'll take you," they said eagerly. "Mrs. Lockerbie will be so happy to spend some time with you." So we arranged a free time, and again I prayed for wisdom.

As the four of us sat in my room, I rejoiced inwardly that God's promise is for where two or three are gathered together in His name—and here we were, four.

I soon learned that Beth was a brand new Christian who had been invited by a friend to attend this retreat, and just about everything was new and strange to her. As we talked, her true problem surfaced. "I do believe in Jesus as my Savior. I did accept Him at the Christian Women's Club. But—" She half-covered her face and gulped, "I *believe,* I think. But then *I don't believe.*"

We let her talk out what she saw as her real problem with being a Christian. Then the incident came to mind of the father who said, "Lord, I believe; help Thou my unbelief."

"Beth," I said, "you aren't the first one to feel as you do,"

109

and I told her in brief about that man in Bible times (and he even *saw* the Lord Jesus and knew of His miracle-working!).

"Jesus didn't rebuke the man for admitting he had unbelief," I assured her.

Then, her tear-filled eyes beginning to light with a glimmer of hope, she said, "Is *that* in the *Bible*!" Meanwhile, I was frantically trying to remember chapter and verse so that Beth could see it for herself. We turned to Mark 9:24.

"Lord, I believe; help thou mine *unbelief*." She read it over and over, aloud; each time looking as though it had been written just for her, to meet her special need. No doubt, you have found from personal experience that the Lord does do that for us. The Bible says, "He knows what things we have need of" (Matthew 6:8). Beth's need was not to feel guilty over not having arrived at a deep level of faith. But she's growing. Her last letter told of victories in her personal life and the joy of winning some of her family to Christ.

TODAY'S THOUGHT: God always has the exact prescription for every need.